"Wise, engaging, and, above all, different."

—Michael Bungay Stanier, *Do More Great Work*

"She tells the truth, straight up. Money, failure, power, appreciation—*The Fire Starter Sessions* doesn't leave anything out of the mix, and Danielle pours it on with **a heaping dose of encouragement and possibility-thinking.**"

—Barbara Stanny, *Overcoming Underearning*

"Danielle's work is jam-packed with keen insights and a force of energy that pushes you in invaluable ways. The content is practical and **ignites the mind in ways that could change your career and life.**"

—Scott Belsky, *Making Ideas Happen*

"Danielle LaPorte is scary smart, yet so kind and practical that she kindles the fire in you without causing you to feel consumed by the flames. She has the knowledge you need to succeed. Lean in and listen close. **What she has to say is what our spirits need to hear.**"

—**Martha Beck,** *Steering by Starlight*

"Danielle is one serious Fire Starter, and you'll be one, too, after reading this masterpiece. For best results, read in your igloo and emerge with a suntan."

—Chris Guillebeau, *The Art of Non-Conformity*

ADVANCE PRAISE FOR *THE FIRE STARTER SESSIONS*

"Danielle's passion leaps off the page, and reading a few chapters of **this book will ignite you into action.**"

—**Gretchen Rubin,** *The Happiness Project*

"A modern masterpiece that will impact millions of lives, for generations to come. It's outrageously inspiring, wise, and actionable. I simply cannot recommend it enough. Prepare for a religious experience. You're going to fall in love with this book."

—Marie Forleo, *www.MarieForleo.com*

"**The revolution you've been waiting for,** it will shake up and wake up every aspect of your life. Danielle LaPorte offers soulful wisdom to create a blueprint for moguls, spiritual rock stars, and lovers of life. Skinny-dip head first into this hot and fabulous book. I dare you."

—**Kris Carr,** *Crazy Sexy Diet*

"The new, badass *Artist's Way.*"

—Linda Sivertsen, *Generation Green*

THE FIRE STARTER SESSIONS

CROWN
ARCHETYPE
NEW YORK

THE FIRE STARTER SESSIONS

A SOULFUL + PRACTICAL GUIDE TO CREATING SUCCESS ON YOUR OWN TERMS

DANIELLE LAPORTE

Published in the United States by Crown Archetype,
an imprint of the Crown Publishing Group, a division
of Random House, Inc., New York.

www.crownpublishing.com

Crown Archetype with colophon is a trademark of Random House, Inc.

Library of Congress Cataloging-in-Publication Data

LaPorte, Danielle,
   The fire starter sessions / Danielle LaPorte. — 1st ed.
      p. cm.
   1. Self-actualization (Psychology) 2. Self-realization. 3. Quality of
work life. 4. Social entrepreneurship. I. Title.

   BF637.S4L358 2012
   158.1—dc23

ISBN 978-0-307-95210-3
eISBN 978-0-307-95212-7

Printed in the United States of America

Book design and jacket design by Maria Elias

10 9 8 7 6 5 4 3 2

First Edition

It is not revolutions and upheavals that clear the road to . . . better days,
but revelations, and lavishness . . . of someone's soul, inspired and ablaze.

—Boris Pasternak, poet

CONNECTING

Everything about the book and extra-hot stuff:

TheFireStarterSessions.com

Connect to my universe here: **DanielleLaPorte.com**

Find me on + Fire Starter reports on Facebook:

www.daniellelaporte.com/facebook

I love Twitter, a lot: **@daniellelaporte**

Twitter hashtag for *The Fire Starter Sessions:* **#FireSS**

Get multidimensional with me—
this is more than a book.

TheFireStarterSessions.com is an extended experience
where you can access:

- *The Workbook o' Fire,* a free downloadable booklet of the worksheet questions from the book.
- *The Camp Fire Guide,* a free guide for creating a book club or group experience.
- *A companion video program, an online community, resource lists . . .* and plenty of other treats and truly useful tools.

CONTENTS

Disclaimers + Admissions   xiii

Come, Sit by the Fire . . .   xv

PART 1
MOJO

Define Yourself on Your Own Terms   3

SESSION 1:
Declare Your Superpowers   20
WORKSHEET: PASSION PLAY   35

SESSION 2:
The Metrics of Ease   40
WORKSHEET: EASY PRIORITIES   54

SESSION 3:
The Strategy of Desire   58
WORKSHEET: CORE DESIRED FEELINGS   73

PART 2
MOXIE

SESSION 4

The Burning Questions   80

WORKSHEET: THE BURNING QUESTIONS   95

SESSION 5

Facing Forward   98

WORKSHEET: PURGE THE PAST URGE   105

WORKSHEET: GLORY BOARDING   107

SESSION 6

Visioneering   110

WORKSHEET: VISION PROMPTING   120

WORKSHEET: DREAM ANALYSIS   121

SESSION 7

Fear + Other Tough Stuff   124

WORKSHEET: DECONSTRUCTING FEAR   136

SESSION 8

Comforting Failure   140

WORKSHEET: COMFORT ZONING   157

SESSION 9

No, Thank You. Yes, Please.   160

WORKSHEET: THE STOP-DOING LIST   173

PART 3
RESULTS

SESSION 10

Make Stuff That Feels Good to Make   178

WORKSHEET: WHAT BUSINESS ARE YOU REALLY IN?   197

SESSION 11

How You Show Up in the World   200

WORKSHEET: THE ALL-ABOUT-YOU INTERVIEW   221

WORKSHEET: THE ASK-A-FRIEND SURVEY   223

SESSION 12

Calling All Sovereigns of Time!   226

WORKSHEET: A PERFECT TWELVE   238

SESSION 13

Money: More Is More. Enough Is Plenty.   242

WORKSHEET: FREELY ASSOCIATING WITH MONEY   271

SESSION 14

Supporting Characters   276

WORKSHEET: SIZING UP SIMPATICO   286

WORKSHEET: SUPPORT TEAM INVENTORY   288

SESSION 15

Be the Giver   292

SESSION 16

Just Start. Now.   304

WORKSHEET: FUTURE GRATITUDE   324

Great, Full   325

The Sonic Fire Playlist   329

Spread the Fire   331

DISCLAIMERS + ADMISSIONS

1. **There is nothing I can give you that you don't already have.** Some of you will find this notion wildly arousing and affirming. *Yeah!* Others may experience instant despair. *What? Isn't this a self-HELP book?* Fret not. We're going to shine a light on the deeply inherent good stuff you have to give—and there's plenty of it.
2. It all comes down to this: **You become a trailblazer by virtue of being your genuine self.** It is that simple—and that profound.
3. I admit it: **I want to be your favorite pyromaniac of clarity, love-fueled ambition, and results.**
4. I may not know you, but **I love you** already. There, I said it.

LoveLove,

Danielle
Xo.

COME, SIT BY THE FIRE . . .

When being real is your priority, the various parts of your life start to groove. Your career will begin to reflect your true passion; your living room will match your values; your friends will fit your soul; and your wealth—of which there are many definitions—will start to measure up with your notion of freedom. Sometimes the courage to be true to yourself comes in the form of an out-loud declaration, a rebellion, or a love-drenched vow. Other times it's a quiet conviction that we can read in your eyes. Mighty or discreet, authenticity is the muscle that helps you shake up beliefs, policies, and restraints, and gives you the strength to do the things some say can't be done. Being genuine is the foundation of integrity—often inconvenient and not always painless—but the only way to go if you're here to really, truly, fully *live*.

Being your true self is the most effective formula for success there is

They don't tell us that in most schools or time management seminars. And not many employee manuals instruct you to:

Be strategic with your desires.
Leverage your contradictions.
Say no to resentment and yes to inspiration.
Make ease a metric of success.

These precepts are kindling for your soul fire, they are the pathways to what you truly want, and they are the reason this book exists.

SOUL FIRE

Our soul fire is ancient and integral to each of us—inextinguishable, but susceptible to being dimmed to faintness. It can get cloaked in layers of self-doubt. We doubt the practicality of enthusiasm and the legitimacy of our impulses. We doubt that breaking the rules will earn us a raise or that speaking in the first person will attract the right clients. We worry that our shine will be construed as showing off and we'll get shot down; or that if we really let our opinions flare, we'll burn bridges that we may need to cross again someday.

Self-doubt is so insidious that it not only renders us stuck in our lives, but it also actually weakens our ability to dream about what living unleashed would look like. And here's the thing: The mere act of dreaming is a vitalizing, life-affirming endeavor. As it turns out, using your imagination is very, very good for your well-being. Einstein believed that imagination was even more important than knowledge itself.

Imagine your ideal life as a mountain of treasures piled high in front of you. It's in the near distance, close enough to walk to on your lunch break. Pile up that mountain o' delight with whatever you want: gold bullion, flat abs, laughing friends, really good times with your family, a career that is bursting with gratification and intrigue, the love of your life, applause and respect, cheers when you cross the finish line, eco-friendly everything, humanitarian relief efforts, the wealth of health, a five-speed coupe with a sunroof, a first-class trip to Monaco, light rays of illumination and peace emanating from you so as to attract devotees or babes (or both). Throw in some multiple orgasms and a fat year-end bonus if that feels good. (That does feel good, right?)

You're standing at a fork in the road. Presumably, both roads will lead to your ideal life. There are two signs pointing to your destination.

One says YOUR WAY.
The other says THEIR WAY.

Which path do you think will be more fun? Never mind about enlightenment or building your credibility. Which path will have more free falls and heart rushes, more laughs, more daring?

If you're thinking that THEIR WAY has some inviting merits, you're right; it does. And I'm not being cynical. THEIR WAY is proven. And "proven" can save you a lot of time and heartache. My role models' victories and bankruptcies, both spiritual and financial, have saved me from expensive mistakes and leveled out my learning curve. The way my soul sisters live their lives deeply influences the choices that I make in my own life. Have you ever said to a friend, in so many words, "Geez, sorry you had to go through that, but now I don't have to. Thanks, man." Among true friends it's obvious that we're learning lessons for one another, sparing each other some pain, eating some karma for team.

You can steer your destiny. You can create the life you want in great detail, but you can't do it alone. THEIR WAY can be very instructive and comforting. And comfort is a beautiful thing when you're risking it all.

But THEIR WAY is an old story. Albeit potentially useful, it's history. It's a myth of experience that we can choose to buy in to or not. Be clear about that. Take what you want from the tried 'n' true archives, and leave the rest. Ultimately, *it's all your call.* Even when stuff seems out of your control, you get to choose how you respond—or react—to everything.

YOUR WAY. Slightly reckless, downright defiant, uncharted, seat-of-the-pants, make it up as you go, not a leg to stand on, what will your mother say? You could bomb. You could become so successful that your friends won't recognize you. (Your real friends always knew you had it in you.) You could break through.

YOUR WAY

The soul fire way.
Ablaze with passion.
Passion that can't be faked.
Passion that the world cannot deny.

DESIRE MORE

This experience—this book and all of the materials on the website—is intended to help you "up" your dreams, to revive or refine them.

I want you to make dream refinement a regular practice. Floss, stretch, eat your greens, dream. And repeat.

Your desires reflect what's truest about you. If your current reality is nowhere close to the life you want, dreams are the fuel that will move you forward. If you want to access your full range of power, then commit to dreaming about your ideal life. Your subconscious and articulated desires are veins of gold that lead to whatever you want to call prosperity.

No matter where you are in your life, whether you're a soaring entrepreneur or an executive in a rut, a student revving up to save the planet or a stay-at-home mom with an identity crisis, an urban shaman wandering or well established, you need to consciously cultivate your dreams. We need to tend to our desires with the same vigilance that we would give to the fire that cooks our food, warms our bones in the night, and keeps the wolves away. Of course, tending to your deep wishes is not a matter of bodily life or death. Without passion, you can still make the rent, be a good guy, and limp along for lifetimes—as many of us do. You'll survive. But we're not here to talk about surviving or justifying just *getting by*. This book is an inquiry into what makes you *thrive*.

IDEALISTS UNITE!

There is nothing more turned on than a person with a dream and the guts to pick up the phone. Dreaming is essential, but it's only part of the equation. You've got to put a strategy into play. (All the overachievers out there are like, *Duh! Milestones, people, milestones!*) Passion is the wind in your sails, and practicality is the rudder. You need both to get where you're going.

As the saying goes, **"The truth is that which works."** You can manage your time like a ninja, make vision boards, and set quarterly goals till the future's so bright you gotta wear shades, but if all those systems don't work, then something's . . . not working. You can meditate till your sit bones are blue, pray, process, train, affirm, think positive, *therapize,* and if you're still not a calmer, more generous person who speaks kindly to the waiter and takes traffic jams in stride, then maybe how you measure the results of your questing needs to be recalibrated.

If your soul fire still looks like it's just flickering in the distance, a mile outside of you, then it's time to consider what gets you hot in the here and now. This may be a radical consideration.

The CEO of a billion-dollar entertainment company once said to me, "There's evolutionary and there's revolutionary. Evolutionary is a degree of change, but *revolutionary* changes everything." He continued, "Take Starbucks, for example. They revolutionized the coffee business. Anyone who follows will be merely evolutionary. And evolutionary is good—it's solid; it can be quite fulfilling. But revolutions! Ah . . . that's the really exciting stuff. Who doesn't want to be revolutionary?! Which would you rather be?"

I'm going for revolutionary, thank you. Not warm—*hot.* Not bright—*blazing.*

The hallmark of revolutionary change is that it beams out to the point of irrepressible, and it affects change in those who witness or experience it. Inward and outward revolutions happen every day. You don't necessarily have to lead a nation to independence or take on the union reps (but by all means . . . if the spirit moves you) . . . A revolution can be a whole new perspective that changes the way you work, achieve wellness, or thrive in a relationship. **A revolution is a way of being that becomes a significantly better way of doing.** And it shifts and lifts people up along with you and keeps the universe on the edge of itself. *A Course in Miracles* defines a miracle as "a shift in perception." Revolutions can feel miraculous.

HEAVY HEART LIFTING

Starting fires and revolutions requires tenacity and faith. And those are hard to come by when you're feeling stuck and spirit fatigued. Spirit fatigue is a malaise with many names: Listlessness. Depression. Incessant resentment. Chronic doubt. Numbness. Feeling small. A persistent fear of loss. Throw in a bad breakup, chemical imbalances, getting downsized, an accident, too much processed food, and the fear-drenched headlines otherwise known as the daily news, and we can veer toward overwhelmed.

When you're physically injured, the rest of your body will make adjustments to compensate for the weakened part. It will carry the brunt in order to endure and carry on, so much so that you don't even notice that the rest of you is knotted up and fatigued. Psychologically we can limp on for years with aching hearts and vexations, just mobile enough to manage day-to-day existence. If you're spirit fatigued for long enough, you will downshift into unconscious enduring. You endure the doubt, and the gray hue, and the disconnectedness. You'll begin to believe that if it's this hard for so many of us, for so long, then that must just be the way it is. And so you make adjustments to your desires. You amend your hopes. You repeatedly ignore your hunger.

When we're spirit-fatigued, we tend to make weak decisions. We compromise. And I'm not talking about the Good Samaritan compromise where you step outside of yourself and do something accommodating for other people. I'm talking about the sell-yourself-short kind of compromise. You know, where you tell yourself that you don't really deserve to want what you want. (*It's so much to ask for.*) That you should be more accommodating. (*It's* *more spiritual to be nice*.) That you really should be more reasonable. (*Logical people are so much more bankable than the emotional types*.) And this killer concept: This is as good as it gets.

These are the very notions that veil the light of your essential self and keep you from what you want the most.

BRAKE FOR PEACE

> I have been running so sweaty my whole life
> Urgent for a finish line
> And I have been missing the rapture this whole time
> Of being forever incomplete
>
> —Alanis Morissette, "Incomplete"

The Path. The Way. The Formula. The Secret. The Answer. The Answer to the Secret. The All-New Way to the Path That Leads to the Secret Formula . . . in Ten Steps or Twenty-one Days—whichever comes first. So many of us are always driving, nonstop, in hopes of arriving at peace, or unshakable confidence, or somewhere further down the street from anxiety. It's the irony of chasing stillness—or trying to get ahead so we can get out of the game. Or of improving ourselves so we can finally accept who we are. It's exhausting.

Humans are gloriously determined to get what they want. We're ridiculously insatiable. We have a propensity for craving—ceaselessly. Buddhists, who are always trying to detach from this wheel of suffering would agree: Constant craving can be a bitch. But on the other end of longing, there is some good news:

Your hunger will lead you home ■

HAPPINESS IS CREATIVE TENSION

The Fire Starter Sessions is like a mixed CD of apathy-kicking sermons and love-soaked questions. We're going to consider the contradictions that make you so gorgeously multidimensional but aren't so easy to reconcile. Your spicy, finicky, idiosyncratic-isms. This tension is where your creativity likes to hang. Tension. Creates.

If we want to live bold, full lives, we must take our whole selves into the future. Nothing can be forsaken or hidden, because it is in integrating all of the aspects of our beings that we expand. Cosmic love *and* worldly ambition, consciousness *and* cash, high standards *and* compassion—this is where it all comes together. And I'll tell you up front that this is really a covert campaign for generosity. Generous, fulfilling outpourings of whatever you've got to give. If you're fully showing up for life, you won't be able to tell the difference between selflessness and self-serving because it feels so good to give . . . or is it receiving?

We're going to get gritty and gracious all in one breath. Success is messy. Career visions spill into lifestyle choices, mash into spiritual paradigms, and ride on top of relationships. It's all interconnected and paradoxical. And promising.

Wisdom comes from embracing contrasting experiences: Lucky breaks and pounding the pavement. A winning streak and a dark night of the soul. Selling out and taking a stand. Wanting it all and walking away.

If wisdom comes from integrating the highs and lows of life, then fulfillment is the result of bringing your whole self to the game. All of you. Not just the politically correct and the well-behaved bits. Not just your master's degree and certifications. And not only your unbounded passion—because putting your passion into form will take all of the mental muscle that you can flex.

IN·TEG·RI·TY *(NOUN)*

1. adherence to ethical principles; soundness of moral character; honesty
2. the state of being whole, entire, or undiminished

If you try to keep your most sacred ambitions off of your weekly calendar

and your most

genuine traits off

of your résumé,

then you're missing

out on the power of

real integrity ■

THE HEAT SOURCE

The Fire Starter Sessions uses career and creativity as levers to expanding your awareness. I don't think you can have a conversation about consciousness without talking about how you show up every day in the world of moneymaking and service. Livelihood is a portal to our personal and collective growth: How we serve, make art, make ends meet. What we earn, how we value ourselves. Work. Labor. Love. Craft. Calling.

As a business and creative strategist, I've worked with hundreds and hundreds of people to help take their visions to the next level. I've done live Fire Starter Sessions with groups in theaters, in boardrooms, on the beach, in living rooms, even in a pole-dancing studio in Los Angeles. I've jammed with a best-selling author who still feels she's living in the shadow of her best-selling father; a Buddhist minimalist who wants to crack six figures a year; a socialite stockbroker who wants to write the next great novel and come out of the closet (not necessarily in that order). I've worked with stay-at-home moms racked with guilt because they're itching to get back to work, and MBAs who want to drop out of the game and make babies. I've worked with marine biologists who want to bring science to the people and the people to the politicians; a sax player on the finer points of commerce meeting art; a surgeon who wants to be a global virtual coach for wellness; and CEOs who want to start over.

I've witnessed life reinventions, joyous emancipation from cubicles, and tripled incomes. I've cheered decisions to walk away from long-term relationships—both professional and romantic—and to tackle piles of emotional and material clutter. I've encouraged people to hold on just a little while longer.

I've watched people give in to fear and rationalize playing it safe. They circle back to the fire, eventually.

I've heard countless "Hell, yes! I'm worth so much more!" revelations. I cherish these epiphanies of self-worth the most, and seeing someone take intelligent steps toward joy, walking away from the obligations and illusions that cramp their heart's desire.

This I know to be true: We are craving to play bigger, to go deeper, to shine.

anything or anyone
that does not bring you alive
is too small for you

—David Whyte, poet

So my beloved Fire Starters, my freedom seekers and fear tamers, in the name of undiminished soul fire and good times, we are gathered here to get clear on what true success truly means to *you*. Let's fan those flames in your heart with colossal and microscopic questions. Let's blaze new trails in your synapses with pondered possibilities and stories of proven courage. Let's turn up the heat on your desires. Because when you set your own light free, you become a veritable force of nature.

part1

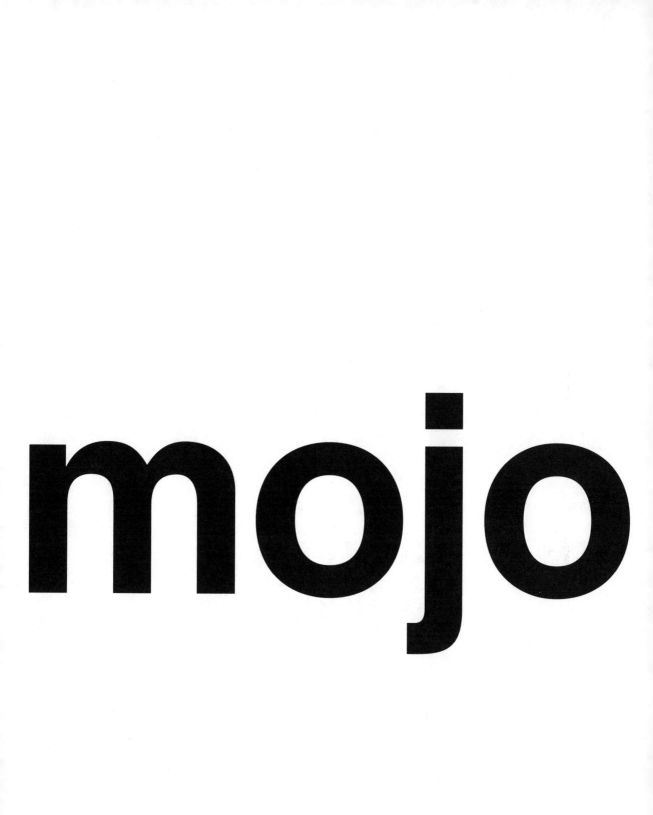

define yourself on your own terms

define yourself on your own terms

I found out that there
weren't too many limitations,
if I did it my way.

—Johnny Cash

THE TRUTH PUNCTUATES

You shouldn't take advice from someone you don't really know, who hasn't dreamed big, or suffered for a spell. Or with whom you haven't experienced at least one major religious holiday. The Sessions that await you abound with righteous persuasions and advice. Thus, you and I should get a bit more acquainted. So before you get to the business of soul unfurling and ambition refining, and taking my word on any of it, allow me to introduce myself by way of a very defining moment in my life.

We had the corner table at JJ Bean café on Commercial Drive and Sixth in Vancouver. There were loan documents, term sheets, and talking points piled next to my peppermint tea. I was looking to Lance, my investor and mentor, to give me some straight-up sage advice. My company was being torn apart by a clash of wills and motives. It was wretched. Everything was on the line: hundreds of thousands of dollars, five years of full-tilt labor and love, long-term relationships, reputations—a very big dream. I had a lawyer (two of them). I had a business coach. I had a Buddhist shrink. What I needed was a friend with hard-core business acumen—someone who knew the ropes and who knew me.

I had that desperate "What should I do?" crease across my fore-head. I was pushing hard for answers, somersaulting over Scenario A or B or . . . Z. Lance made it clear, with his eyes twinkling. He said:

"You're freer than you think you are."

You must be kidding me. Free? I'd never felt so trapped in my life. The pressure was a whole new phenomenon in my nervous system. Bankers were calling my cell phone, investors were having clandestine meetings without me, and my once beloved business partner and I hadn't spoken to each other in months. . . .

TRIAL BY FIRE:
HOW I GOT HERE

I have a degree in faking it till you make it. I earned it, and then I burned it. In 2000, I was wearing a black suit and loafers, with a straight bob haircut. As executive director of a Washington, D.C.–based think tank of world-class futurists, I shopped white papers to the Pentagon and the World Bank. I wrangled an incredible team of quirky, Mensa-level thinkers to surmise and analyze potential outcomes for the AIDS epidemic in Africa, possible global water shortages, chaotic social meltdowns . . . and stuff like that. In terms of think tanks, it was Candy Land. Smart, fast-moving, and funded. Almost daily I was asked where I went to college (I didn't), and to sign yet another nondisclosure agreement (which I did). From nine to five, I read about weapons of mass destruction and scenario planning; on weekends, it was Rilke's poetry, Jiddu Krishnamurti's theology, and the latest *Rolling Stone*.

James Carville said that "D.C. is Hollywood for ugly people." Think tanks are a bit glam in the Capitol. But behind my title and White House security pass, I was managing a raging impostor complex. I craved pop culture and mysticism. My, uh, *progressive* attitude clashed with the policies and posturing that is the fabric of the political scene. In my first month in town, I showed up to a White House meeting with purple streaks in my hair. I may as well have flashed a KGB badge when I pulled up to the table. The meeting chair took me aside afterward. "You're not from here, are you?" he said with a wink.

I was learning a lot, but mostly I was wilting inside. Eventually I resigned. More accurately, I fled, back to my homeland, burned out and confused. I looked at my loafers and thought, "Who the hell bought *those*?" I schlepped my suits to the consignment store, dyed my hair bright red, pierced my nose, and got some new tattoos. Naturally.

Then came the inevitable identity crisis and searching. There was a sojourn to India for a private meeting with the Dalai Lama, time in ashrams and retreat centers, tea with Eckhart Tolle. In order to make the rent, I revived my old communications and publicity agency "for visionary people and projects," and I did what I swore I'd never do again: hustled other people's ideas to jaded television producers and radio show hosts. Meanwhile, some friends and I were plotting to raise a million bucks to open an urban spa-meets-yoga-studio-meets-community-center-meets-organic-restaurant-meets-boutique (and we could franchise!). Then I woke up to the obvious fact that I didn't want to do anything that involved having a set of master keys or giving staff performance reviews. I tried to get into art school. I still have that rejection letter.

And then a new opportunity presented itself. After months of wandering and awkward networking, I joined forces with a hard-working friend who had a good idea. She had the inspired concept, I had the brains for getting stuff out the door, and we both had a lotta style. We quickly and successfully launched what could most simply be called an image consultancy company . . . with soul.

This was a quantum leap toward my truer calling. I was wearing linen tunics and twisted my hair into dreadlocks. We raised hundreds of thousands of dollars in investment capital and hired a hotshot

CEO to run the show. I wrote our flagship book, and my partner art directed it. *The Oprah Show* producers called. Magazines flew in photographers to take our picture. Major TV networks romanced us. Our site traffic climbed exponentially—just what we desired. We were headed to what we wanted to be: rich 'n' famous, and fast. But profit and status began to lead the charge, and our slogan, "inspire authenticity," became tragically . . . inauthentic.

Every day before I walked into our stylin' studio office with its glossy white walls and big abstract art, I had to psych myself up for the creative tension that awaited me, the strife that would eventually flatten our little empire. A sunny Monday morning. My hand on the doorknob next to a plaque with my name on it. I took a deep breath before I opened the door. *You can do this,* I said to myself. Quickly followed by the thought, *This is so utterly fucked.* Apply a smile and enter stage left: "Good morning, everybody." This grin 'n' bear it entry into the day got to be a habit.

I became increasingly quiet as more opinions about how we should grow the company got added to the mix. There was a lot of money on the line for a lot of people, like the friends who had chipped in a month's salary to become investors, and the various venture capitalists who wrote six-figure checks. The dream was big, and I wasn't going to sound the alarms with my abstract and unquantifiable concerns that things *just didn't feel right.* I didn't think that lack of laughter in the office would be considered a key data point for the investors. The day I gave over signing authority on the company bank account, I wanted to scream, "This is wrong! Very, very wrong. May the Goddess of Creative Justice enforce her wrath, thereby righting this perturbation in the very depths of my soul!" But that would have been so, you know, *dramatic.* Instead, I said nothing. We had obligations now, and I was going to be democratic, responsible, shrewd, and all kinds of flexible in order to make good on those promises.

Shortly before it all imploded my business partner and I did a video interview with a high-profile business website. We lied like rugs. "Yes, thank you, it *is* so great to inspire thousands of women every week to live more authentically." Then I think we threw in some bullshit about the thrill of being entrepreneurs and how we wouldn't have it any other way. When we wrapped the segment, I raced to unclip my mic like I was shaking a snake off my neck.

The next day the program tech called with profuse apologies. "I'm so sorry. This has never happened before, but the video file got corrupted somehow. We're so embarrassed with the technical snafu. Can we please set up for a reshoot?" he pleaded. *There is a God,* I sighed. I was so relieved that my lying ass wasn't going to be immortalized on YouTube. I suggested to the producer that we re-film in a few months. I was just buying time. I could feel something coming. The following week, it would all be over for me.

Our CEO took us to the corner café for one of our regular check-in meetings. But this meeting was going to be extraspecial, because it would be the last time I'd ever see him. Apparently it had been decided (I say *apparently* because neither my cofounder nor I was involved in the decision) that a new business model would be more beneficial for the company. It sounded something like this:

I was given the option to take a small percentage of my salary (woo!) and to write a blog post or two a week—from home (fun!). I didn't need to be told that the business owned all of my stuff. I'd made myself an employee of the company—which was not my company anymore. Every photograph of me that was ever taken, every single article I posted, royalties on the book I wrote, intellectual property from the consulting service—even my Twitter identity—all of it, not owned by me. It didn't matter that my name was on the door or in the dot-com. Clearly, I was dismissed. My partner was made a similar kind of offer, which I guess she went for. (I say *guess* because at about that point, after talking almost daily for years, we stopped speaking.)

As the news was being delivered, I didn't flinch. My body was so flooded with endorphins of rage that my freeze instinct kicked in and prevented me from shaking uncontrollably or lunging across the table. I vaguely remember wondering if there was a sharp object within reach. I clenched my jaw and fixed my gaze. I consciously slowed down my breathing to cool the boiling I felt behind my face and in my chest. I delivered my parting words from the café with steely calm: "Thanks for the information. I know all that I need to know." I stormed back to the studio, folded up my laptop, and burned rubber out of my parking space. Driving home that day, I screamed so loud in the car that my voice was hoarse by the time I walked in the door, my face mascara streaked, my body trembling.

And yet . . . even through the noise of shock and brokenheart-edess, I could hear a still and present voice within my being, and it was saying, "*Yes. Finally.*"

YOUR BODY KNOWS

I've heard of a Japanese mogul who lets his meal choices guide his business decisions. While he's eating dinner he thinks about or discusses the business proposition of the day. If he digests it well, he takes positive action. If the meal doesn't go down well, then the deal doesn't go down, either.

My stomach was throwing me cues along the way. The truth was in the breath I held back with my opinions. But I ignored the persistent pinch of raw nerves and regular heavy-headedness. I struck bargains with my resentment and longings. And in doing so,

I betrayed myself. The theatrical deception of my fellow actors was a manifestation of that. Thank the Lord that it was all over in one fell swoop. No matter how long coming, emancipation feels swift and merciful when she shows up.

Which brings us back to the corner table at JJ Bean's café with peppermint tea and Lance on a rescue mission. . . .

"Look, you're in the jungle. So just play by the rules of the jungle." Lance leaned in. "It's time for you to take care of yourself, Danielle. You got yourself into this mess because you gave away your power. This is your chance to get the lesson. I want you to get this one so you never repeat it again. Jungle rules. Power rules." You know, those pesky, repeating lessons.

Got it. Free. In the jungle. *Merowww*. This lesson was deeper for me than angel mentor man could have known.

"I get it. I do," I said. "I get that there're some bogus propositions on the table. They're trying to bully me. This is jungle shit and it's piled high, I know, I know." I pressed on. The furrow in my brow was going to need Botox soon. "But, if I exercise my legal rights—and I know I'm on seriously solid ground here—if I decide to get all kung fu on this, then some people could lose their houses and have their credit trashed. I know playing 'fair' will cost me a lot of money—money that I don't have. Yet." I doodled nothingness on the paper in front of me. I continued, "They can kiss my ass on Main Street, but I don't want to wreck any lives here. There's gotta be a way . . ." My voice trailed off. I looked out the window and saw a smiling Rasta dude riding by on a bicycle. *I wonder if that guy has the answer,* I thought.

And then my mentor broke the silence and said it—gently, but emphatically. Kindly, but deadly serious: **"Are you an entrepreneur, or what?"**

It was question, not a criticism. And it hung in the air like a sword over a sacrificial altar. I think I heard tribal drums *b-b-beating* in the background. It was a test. Door #1: Self-respect. Self-reliance. Define myself on my own terms. Door #2: Keep the respect of the very rich, highly intelligent, truly helpful investor guy. And very rich, highly intelligent, truly helpful investor guys are not the kinds of people you want to burn bridges with. And besides, I was adoringly grateful to him for everything. I was rather compelled to get the answer to his question right.

Jungle rules. Eat or be eaten. Bite back. Take no prisoners.

My career flashed through my mind like freeway exits zipping by. Lemonade stand at age eight—profitable; lobbied to sell tickets to the school carnival (*Parents should pay double*); talked bankers into better rates and investors into investing (*We're the next big thing*); major magazine spreads and thousands of click-throughs; hired, fired, and then hired some more; IP, CEO, COO; worked miracles by COB to get a ROI. Of course I'm an . . . entrepreneur. Or am I?

> I am not the person who is singing
> I am the silent one inside. . . .
> I am not my house, my car, my songs
> They are only stops along my way. . . .
>
> —Paula Cole, "Me"

And then I got it. This wasn't my definition of me—not entirely. I took a deep breath and let the pause gestate. I was prepared for Lance to leave the table, to tell me I was a hopeless romantic, unfit to rule any dynasty. *Nice knowing you, softy*. My truth had occurred to me, finally, undeniably.

So I admitted it: "I'm a humanitarian." And then I put a fine point on it: "Who happens to be an entrepreneur." And then I really declared it. "And I think I can protect myself without fucking anyone else over."

Relief. In that moment, I was okay if Lance walked out on me, because something inside me had clicked into its rightful place: ruthless compassion. Yes, I was done suffering fools. No, I would not make pretty, spiritualized excuses for anyone's bad behavior anymore—mine included. I would put on my own oxygen mask first. I would stand in my very immense power. And I would aim to do it free of vengeance, free of resentment, grateful for all that I had. Inside, I was purring like a panther in her tree. Smiling.

I must have passed the test because Lance smiled right back at me. "Well, fine. That's all we needed to know," he said, with grounded glee. "Then here's what a humanitarian entrepreneur should do . . ."

And from there, we mapped out my future. Love, jungle rules, and all.

As for that ol' company of mine? Well they started running articles on cellulite cream and pregnant brides (nothing against pregnant brides—my mother was one). And they soon went bust. Karma. Dharma. *Duh*. Everyone involved went on to do what they were meant to.

I became a Fire Starter.

CREATIVE SPIRIT IS FREE

I rode the Metro in Washington, D.C., for three years, and all it takes is one week sandwiched between depressed and frazzled government commuters in their too-tight Dress Shed suits and crappy ties, eating things in wrappers, looking vacantly into the dark tunnel, to conclude that *Yep, nine to five can be a special kind of hell.*

Around that time I came into a lot of contact with military and Pentagon folk in the work I was doing. As a vegetarian, apolitical Canadian with crystals tucked into my bra and the Law of Attraction as my secret weapon, I wasn't too stoked to meet any colonels back then. I reeked of judgment. But now I can tell you from experience that the Pentagon is peppered with enlightened folks whose primary intention is to actually make the world a more peaceful place. They believe in universal intelligence and they're remarkably open-minded. So the joke was on me. The human spirit thrives everywhere.

And the entrepreneurial spirit thrives everywhere—even in cubicles and on factory lines.

Since before the Pentagon days, I've been waving the great freedom flag of working for yourself. *Bust out! Crush restrictions! Creative reign or death!* I'm a midwife of the strategies that make freedom dreams real—and proud as any Baptist or marine about it. Righteousness is beautiful, dangerous territory.

Thanks to social media there are so many of us screw-the-system cool kids with platforms now—big blogs and subscriber lists, best-selling books and popular talks—and the potential for superiority and divisiveness is cropping up. Jobs versus Careers. Ninjas versus Suits. Artists versus Civil Servants.

Is someone working at ABC Tool & Die missing out on the good life? Are line workers and nine-to-fivers less daring, less free, less . . . entrepreneurial? I know VPs of marketing who are profoundly liberated in how they bring their talents and skills to the world. And I know a lot of people who work for themselves in such a punishing way that they may as well be working for The Man.

It's not about the packaging. It's not about the form. It's the heart of the matter that we need to see.

It's the creative spirit that I want to foster. Inside the system and out. Everywhere.

Mike Rowe, host of the Discovery Channel show *Dirty Jobs,* sums it up in a fabulous TEDTalk he gives on the war on work. His masterfully told story begins with a tale of castrating sheep, winds through some Greek philosophy, and lands on this insight: "Clean and dirty aren't opposites; they are two sides of the same coin. Just like innovation and imitation, risk and responsibility."

When we peel back the labels and the job titles and being cool, all forms of work and art are an opportunity for liberation and contribution.

It doesn't really matter where you are on the scale of entrepreneurial drive, or if you're in the jungle with a machete or a butter knife. You can call it a hobby, a labor of love, or a world domination plan. You can compete. You can go with the flow.

You can call it ambition, hunger, inspiration, drive, avocation, or putting food on the table. You can crush the competition, unite the people, or change just one person's life. You can falter.

The bottom line is this: If you want to make lots of really good stuff happen in your life, then that's really exciting—for all of us. If you want to earn a living by doing meaningful things, then that makes you exceptional.

This truth is most evident: In seeking our freedom, we liberate our potential to accomplish incredible things.

As people with the creative spirit, we're obsessed with possibility. We live for the rush of turning a thought —an abstract idea— into something real, tangible, touchable, readable, effectual,

profitable. We feel

empowered, generous

even, in the making

of our art. We have

a practical indignation

for mediocrity. We love

to get things done ■

original zone

second nature

transcendental

innate gift

giving of

you

SESSION 1

declare your super-powers

Forget about good.
Good is a known quantity.
Good is what we all agree on.
As long as you stick to good,
you'll never have real growth.

—Bruce Mau, designer

COMPETENCY IS FOR SUCKERS

You're probably incredibly, thoroughly competent at a number of things. You track down the best deal on flights, you know how to cook a turkey, your digital photos are organized, you know enough Spanish to get back-road directions in Oaxaca. You actually know how to pronounce Oaxaca. You hire, fire, charm loan officers, and change printer cartridges before most people have put the cream in their first coffee. You're on top of it.

I used to tell my staff, **"Be careful what you're good at—you could end up doing it for years."** Take Ginger. She started working for me as a bookkeeper. When she came on board, receipts bulged out of tattered envelopes, tax time was looming, and I was playing one credit card off the other (a science in and of itself, as many start-up founders will attest).

Ginger was very competent, and she was as earnest and committed as the day is long. She sorted out the mess, set up maintainable systems, and even brought tulips into the office. Over time, it became radiantly clear that hiding behind Ginger's calculator was her great, creative mind. She came up with story ideas; she made connections to the brand and the market that we hadn't yet articulated. She thought in terms of multimedia and repurposing. She shone when we pulled her into jam sessions.

Eventually the business outgrew her bookkeeping skills and we needed to outsource to a company with a wider skill set (and faster; Ginger was never in a big rush). By that time, we had enough cash flow to pay her to contribute to the creative side of things. During the transition, she responsibly volunteered to keep doing the books until we found a suitable new money manager. "No!" I blurted out. "Just because you can, doesn't mean you should."

"How would it feel if you never touched another receipt again?" I asked her.

"Fucking amazing," she confirmed. Consider it done. I dare posit that saying *good-bye* to competent and *hello* to getting paid to be her naturally talented self might have been the happiest day of Ginger's professional life.

If it doesn't light you up, you're not the right person for the job.

Legendary choreographer Twyla Tharp uses the athlete as a metaphor for this kind of refinement. The talented sports guy has to weigh out many factors: "What comes naturally to him, what does he enjoy the most, in which sport does he have a natural advantage? **But in the end the choice should be based on pure instinct and self-knowledge.** What sport does he feel in his muscles and bones? What sport was he born to play?"

Would you rather be sufficient or masterful?
Would you rather be bright or a freaking supernova?
Would you rather be well-rounded or on your own leading edge?

Your most valuable currency is what comes most naturally to you. Cash in ■

Pure instinct and self-knowledge. If these are our guide points, then we must hold firm to what gives us joy, and in doing so, **we ourselves become the dispensers of joy.** The *I Ching* puts it this way: "The way of the Creative is to win others' hearts through following the truth within ourselves." Score one for sincerity and courage.

THE PRIVILEGE OF A LIFETIME

If poetry does not come as naturally as leaves to a tree, then it had better not come at all.

—John Keats

I'll always remember a Bruce Springsteen interview I saw on MTV in the eighties. The Boss was hitting his zenith of success. *Born in the USA* had nonstop radio play; people were lining up days in advance to buy concert tickets. In the interview, the VJ was asking Bruce about his mega album sales and growing fortune. Jersey smooth and humble as ever, he just shook his head. "You know, man, I just can't believe I get paid for doin' somethin' that comes so natural to me"—he paused—"with so much love."

I want what he's got! I thought. I want my fortune to be who I am. I want it to be *that easy*.

And that's the stride—the life cycle of talent and return that I've been angling for my whole working life. I want the "privilege of a lifetime," as Joseph Campbell called it, "of being myself."

Once upon a time, I thought being well-rounded was the aim of the game. I wanted to be able to work any room, to be the first pick for every team, to know enough to impress anybody I sat next to in business class or partied with at a rave. I pushed myself to keep up with what was happening in the Middle East and New York Fashion Week. When my boss said I needed to master QuickBooks to be a "more well-rounded" member of the team, I pulled all-nighters to figure it out. Another boss told me I needed to be more restrained, yet more outspoken. (Huh?)

One boss actually said to me, as if I should be charged with grand theft auto, "You know, Danielle, you just want to do what you're good at." The nerve of me! Lock me up without Wi-Fi. Just a few more years in this delusional business system and I'll get over those pesky urges for self-gratification. Fo' sho'.

I constantly weighed my every opinion, always scanning for the right time to insert myself into conversations. Hemmed in. Folded.

I do not want to be folded
for where I am folded,
there I am a lie.

—Rilke

I tried to become adept at bookkeeping, cooking, sewing. (I initially pursued a career in fashion design, until I noticed that I had raging headaches every time I sewed or pieced together a pattern. Loved the fashion, hated the construction.) I tried to brush up on my knowledge of wine, new physics, and the predictable interpersonal dynamics of teams. It was an anxiety-inducing curriculum of people pleasing. Identity Refinement 101. Subtle panic.

Eventually, I started giving up trying to be good at stuff that made me feel bad. Not because I was becoming more enlightened or daring, but because I was getting worn out. Task by task, attitude by attitude. The things that were fun and joy inducing in my career were getting harder to resist—begging for my fuller attention. I learned what it meant to pick my battles, and I couldn't bear to battle with my instincts anymore. I wanted to feel in sync with The Force, not at odds with it. "Up for a challenge" was no longer cool—it was mostly a hassle. I stopped criticizing myself for not being enthusiastic about learning certain things. Getting shit from bosses proved to be entirely unavoidable, so, eventually, I got back to being my own boss.

Every admission about the things I loathed to do felt like a giant step forward for deeply ambitious humans everywhere.

Screw Excel! It's ugly and inflexible. I'd rather figure out how to make thousands of dollars than how to count the pennies. I want to lead people, not manage them. Most team meetings are flatlining and unproductive. Count me out.

Of course I second-guessed myself, as one tends to do on the cusp of transformation. I was actually pretty *decent* at figuring out IT systems and making them work. I was *good* at motivating staff and getting the best out of people. I was a *fair* meeting dominatrix and could get priorities outlined with lightning speed. I was generally very *competent,* thank you very much. Couldn't competent counterbalance the lackluster feelings? Wasn't the grind part and parcel of being a grown-up?

I began to notice I was attracted to eccentrics, crazy obsessive fanatics who immersed themselves in their creative worlds. I really liked people who admitted when they didn't know something, "Out of my league—no idea." What a refreshingly real response in contrast to the bullshit, empty-eyed refrains of know-it-all answers and feigned interest. Specialists intrigued me. Enthusiasts made me swoon. I wanted to be one of those Passionate People. One of Kerouac's "mad ones": "the ones who are . . . desirous of everything at the same time, the ones that never yawn or say a commonplace thing, but burn, burn, burn like fabulous yellow Roman candles exploding like spiders across the stars . . ." Slam. Poetry.

A chilled-out but insistent voice kept reminding me: "You didn't sign up for good enough in this lifetime, you signed up for *awesome*." Right. Got it. Awesome. And I deftly concluded:

Being well-rounded is highly overrated ◼

Who are you trying to impress?

What do you have to force yourself to do?

What would you like to never, ever do again?

APPROVE OF YOUR WEAKNESSES

If you've got the strength and pride to fly your superhero flag, then you also have the mettle to admit to what you suck at. Such admissions have lasting benefits.

WHEN YOU COP TO YOUR SHORTCOMINGS

- You become accessible. Humanity is charming. *What, you're not superhuman? Well then let's be friends.*
- You make space for other people to perform, shine, and operate from their true strengths—a living inspiration.
- You foster teamwork and collaboration.
- You get the benefit of other people's greatness.
- You create a genuine connection.
- You get help. People support you.
- You actually don't have to do it all. Go figure.
- You give yourself permission to pursue your genius.

AU NATUREL

Jonathan Livingston Seagull . . . was no ordinary bird. Most gulls don't bother to learn more than the simplest facts of flight—how to get from shore to food and back again. For most gulls, it is not flying that matters, but eating. For this gull, though, it was not eating that mattered, but flight. More than anything else, Jonathan Livingston Seagull loved to fly.

—Richard Bach, *Jonathan Livingston Seagull*

When you focus on building your natural strengths and doing what comes easiest to you, you gain a momentum in your life that feels efficient and exciting and hot. Like, sexy kind of hot, and deeply nourishing kind of hot; like your heart on fire kind of hot. The kind of hot we all want to feel. Are you with me?

True strength is not necessarily about skill or adeptness. It's about vitality. Holding this perspective changes everything, my friend. And it goes back to my root theory in life—that our actions are driven by our desire. It means that all that stuff that you may be good at but don't *really* love to do, you get to dump . . . mostly. No more faking it to make it.

With his books *Now, Discover Your Strengths* and *The Truth About You,* Marcus Buckingham is a true-strengths zealot. He puts it this way: "A strength is what you do that makes you feel strengthened." Boom. So it's not necessarily what you're good at or what you're capable of—it's what feels amazing when you do it. Ergo, a weakness is the stuff you do that makes you feel weakened. Deceptively simple. Revolutionary.

According to Buckingham—and I couldn't agree more—we will never be great at the things we have to try to be good at. But we can be amazing at the things we're easily great at. I vote for outstanding. Can I get a witness?

When my awesomesaucey son was about four years old, we went to a local ice cream parlor for a treat. It was a soft summer evening, just perfectly perfect, and we sat in the parlor's garden, under twinkly lights, licking our cones, not saying much. "So, Monkey," I said through chocolate licks, "what's it feel like to be alive, like, *how's your life*?" And without missing a beat, and with a slight cowboy lilt, he replied, "Oh, Mama! It's ahhh-MAZing. If I were a telephone, I'd be ringin' all the time!" Attaboy.

WORK YOUR PASSION

Masters focus on what they do best. That's how they become masters. They stay in their zone, and the zone is what feels good. Damn good.

So what about good, old-fashioned sweat and determination? It's essential, of course. But there is a remarkable difference in slogging to fit the bill and pushing yourself to break the mold. There's *being obligated* to run hard versus *wanting* to run hard. There's duty, and there's passion. And you can't fake passion.

Passion will always move you in the direction of your authentic self.

Passion guarantees you a place in the hero's journey action course. It helps you know what to say yes or no to. No more trying to be a marketing genius when what you do best is negotiating with vendors or pumping up the sales team—hire a PR genius. No more faking that you love to cook so you'll look like a better parent or partner. Give yourself permission to keep it basic. (And count me in. Most meals at my house are picnics in the living room.) No more trying to come up with blue-sky, five-year plans when you're a short-term, focused-details guy—get a coach or a visionary friend to help you see the big possibilities.

And, by the way, passion doesn't need to be constantly fiery and all consuming; it can be a steady curiosity and commitment. You don't need to want to die for your calling or chain yourself to a tree for your cause. **Genuine curiosity** and sincere interest are burning coals that can warm you for a good, long time.

Your curiosity is your growth point. Always.

FOR THE LOVE OF LIGHT

When do you feel ahhh-MAZing?

What makes you *ring*?!

What activities cause you to feel useful, vital, better than before?

When do you have that "there's more where that came from" feeling?

What feels so good and so easy to give that you give it generously?

What do you do best—that gives you a rush while you're doing it?

What lights your fire?

You grow most in your areas of greatest strength. You will improve the most, be the most creative, be the most inquisitive, and bounce back the fastest in those areas where you have already shown some natural advantage over everyone else—your strengths. This doesn't mean you should ignore your weaknesses. It just means you'll grow most where you're already strong.

—Marcus Buckingham, *Now, Discover Your Strengths*

This is akin to what Stephen Covey called "sharpening your saw" in his oldie but goody, *The 7 Habits of Highly Effective People.* I adore this concept: **Get better at what you're best at.**

Go deeper. When you deepen your interests and stretch your talents, the world feels bigger and full of even more promise. You'll be able to see more, grasp more, catch the nuances of your psyche, and make connections with the greater whole. When you're honoring your own drive, you'll be more compassionate. And, ironically, when you strive for mastery, you become more accessible. Aspiring to something greater always makes you more vulnerable. And it's that kind of openness that allows for learning to occur.

I try to collaborate with people who operate from their zone of true strengths so that I can learn from the best—from people who are *being* their best. And so I can be seen and called out and polished up when I'm shrinking, faking, or faltering.

HOW CAN YOU TELL IF SOMEONE IS IN THEIR ZONE?

They show up because they're compelled to—they can hardly resist.

They ask really good questions because they're always scanning for the right fit.

They're really comfortable saying no to things that pull
   them away from what they love.
They're incredibly generous.
They look you in the eye.

INVEST IN YOUR
SECOND NATURE

**Your original self and all its great capacities are present from
day one.**

Jungian analyst James Hillman calls it "the acorn theory." It is
the idea that we are born with a soul that shapes our destiny—that
our full potential already lives within us. That potential may lie dormant until your life conditions become the ideal environment for you
to sprout . . . until you're big enough to run the race, or you have
the vocabulary to better argue your point, or until the right teacher
comes along to stretch your mind to its fuller proportions.

For some of us, growth-conducive circumstances happen in
childhood thanks to both inner talent and outer surroundings. It can
be difficult to tell which comes first—the talent or the conditions.
Take Venus and Serena Williams, for example, whose father had
visions of Wimbledon trophy plates for his babies and had them
swinging tennis rackets as soon as they could walk. For others,
the lightning flash of potential might not show up until later in life.
Diana Krall, one the world's best-selling jazz artists, didn't start
singing until she was twenty-six. The literary virtuoso Colette didn't
pick up a pen to write fiction until she was more than fifty.

Hillman explains: "The acorn theory expresses that unique

something that we carry into the world, that is particular to us." It is connected to our *daimon,* a Greek word scarcely used in our culture, which loosely translates to "inner voice." The Roman word was *genius*, and the Christian word is *guardian angel*. What if instead of looking to our genes, our social class, or the expectations of the household we grew up in, our whole educational system focused on each child discovering his or her very own daimon? The model would be one of eliciting and evoking, rather than molding and configuring. What if every individual was considered a mystery to observe and support, rather than a vessel to fill with outside information?

Can you remember who you were, before the world told you who you should be?

NORMAL IS BORING

The need to be normal is the predominant anxiety disorder in modern life.

—Thomas Moore, *Original Self*

Naturally driven excellence is not "normal," by the way. Most amazing people are a tad eccentric or obsessive. A little off-kilter. Driven. Devoted. (Nowhere in the definition of *devoted* do the words *balanced, measured,* or *normal* appear.) Freaky excellent people do not have subtle strengths, they have *pronounced* talents or proclivities, and they have a rabid dedication, a flaming ardor for what they do so well. They dig it, and they dig it hard.

Though unmitigated, unapologetic stupendousness is the exception rather than the norm in our culture, champions of authenticity can be found in every profession or calling. Bakers, day-care teachers, technologists, activists—everyone has some form of genius to rock. And when you're letting your genius fly, you make it look so natural. Because it is.

PASSION PLAY

WORKSHEET

Your true strengths are living right *here.*

What are you intensely interested in? While you're at it, include your moderate curiosities.

You go to the best cocktail party ever. It's a life-changing event because you meet the most with-it, interesting, empowered people, and each of them can contribute to your career and interests in some way. . . . Who was there? What kind of information did they share with you? What did they ask you? How did they offer to help you?

If you could go to five conferences or events this year, which ones would you go to, or what would they be about?

What could you talk about late into the night with like-minded people without running out of things to say?

What activities make you feel really useful, alive, and strong? When do you feel like a rock star, a gifted contributor, a very cool and purposeful human being? In terms of things that you do, when do you feel most like yourself?

What do you want to be known for?

Be you,

be true,

be strong ■

A WORD ON LIFE PURPOSE

So many people are looking for it: their Big Life Purpose.

Becoming YOU is your purpose.

YOU are the very purpose of your existence. Realizing what lights your fire and floats your boat—that's your life purpose. What else could it be?

If it gives you true joy (not the seemingly happy high that is fleeting, but the reliable, always-there kind of satisfaction) to rock that guitar, to make people laugh, to discover the world, to make things a little more beautiful wherever you go, to feed, to stir it up, to clean it up, to execute the plan, to bank the cash, to be a compassionate citizen, to explore nonstop, or purely to seek pleasure . . . then, that's your life purpose!

Your life purpose is what you say it is.

Who could tell you otherwise?

grace simplicity

easy breezy

least resistance

obvious play

smooth sailing

relaxed

trusting

yes

SESSION 2

the
metrics
of ease

An integral being knows without going,
sees without looking, and accomplishes without doing.

—Lao-tzu

Take a nap
Making the mountain water
Pound the rice.

— Kobayashi Issa

What would your life be like if you did only what was easy?

Let me repeat the question:

What would your life be like if you did only what was easy? ■

It's almost unsettling to go there, isn't it? When I try to answer that question for myself, I squirm a bit. Lazy dilettante. *As if.* What would I do with all that extra time I'd have if I just did the easy stuff? Hmmm . . . maybe I'd have more time to enjoy what I've got and get more of what I want. Maybe things would be . . . easier.

Ease. The concept confounds most of us. Here's why:

Pay your dues. Put in your time. Prove yourself. Check the right box. Stay the course. Meet expectations. Soldier on. Nothing worthwhile comes easily. Good things come to those who wait. Blue collar, white collar, hard work pays off. No pain, no gain. Thomas Edison put it this way: *There is no substitute for hard work.*

We'll call these, collectively, the Myth of Endurance: a concept that you can choose to believe in, in varying degrees, or not. "Easy" is also a concept that can be just as useful to you. The easy way is a direction that leads to spacious places.

Choosing easy is smart, efficient, elegant; a fantastic form of self-compassion; giving yourself a break and getting out of your own way. Choosing easy is letting inspiration be your compass. Choosing easy is allowing for the things that you've been asking for to enter your life.

Now, let's be clear, there are two types of easy. Quality easy and cheap easy. We're aiming for Quality, with a capital Q.

THE QUALITY KIND OF EASY

Quality easy has a sense of fluidity to it. There's a gravitational pull *forward*. Quality easy relies on his inner strength. Quality easy has an abiding respect for herself.

Quality easy has fewer things on the to-do list and is a brilliant delegator. Quality easy trusts the timing of things. He knows it's better to hold out for what's right than to deal with the mess of extracting himself from a bad compromise. The minute resentment and irritation set in to a task, Quality easy goes on red alert. She steers clear of aggravation, annoyance, and repetitive misery. Over time, Quality easy gets comfortable saying *no, thank you,* to things that are just too complicated and too distant from what she really wants. She is willing to let it go, get over it, and walk away—because she has better things to do with her life energy. It's that simple, most of the time.

Quality easy brings **a sense of expansion** to things. Quality easy is compelling—because when you say yes to grace, you're saying yes to the natural flow of life. You lift your face toward the divine, like flowers lean into the light.

THE CHEAP KIND OF EASY

Cheap is a sucker for a discount. Cheap easy can't see that some losses are gains. Cheap easy stays in a stifling relationship because it seems easier than facing the heartbreak and dividing up the furniture. Cheap easy is frequently in a rush, a smidge desperate, and usually scrambling for options. Cheap easy tells little white lies to get things done.

The path of least resistance isn't about shortcuts, cutting corners, or being clever. And it's certainly not about making mediocrity acceptable. It's about optimizing the truth. It's about casting your seeds on the most fertile soil for your best chances for success.

START WITH THE EASY STUFF

Easy is sublimely logical. Consider all of the things you want to create, produce, accomplish, put out in the world, and experience—so many roads that could lead to satisfaction. Start with the project or the aspect of the project that is the easiest. What do you already know the most about? Where are there already ambassadorships and alliances? What are people already asking you for?

The same goes for creating satisfying relationships. What's already going well that you can lean in to? What do you adore about the other person that you can focus on? The easy stuff is right in front of you and totally doable: simple kindnesses freely given day to day. Start there and you can approach the big hairy issues with some lightness.

Instant gratification has gotten a bad rap. I'm all for it. **Why would you want to delay gratification?** Within the constraints of morality and maturity, you should do whatever you need to do to feel gratified in the moment. It may be as subtle as choosing a more positive thought or reminding yourself to smile. Maybe it's taking two minutes in your car or at your desk to do nothing but just feel into the day. Maybe instant gratification is fifty sit-ups for an adrenaline rush, ordering dessert first, giving an unexpected hug, signing the lease, or telling your boss to shove it. You can be responsible to those around you while creating immediate pleasure for yourself.

Pleasure makes everything easier. Gratification builds the momentum, motivation, and muscle for you to choose the work ahead of you that will require more patience and stamina. It warms you up to shine.

My creativity coach and friend Dyana Valentine is an ambassador of the easy way. "If it doesn't feel easy and juicy, then you're automatically dropping your operation percentage down to about 80 to 70 percent." She's 100 percent right.

Easy is

productive ■

Less friction = greater velocity. When you start with the easy stuff, you foster optimism. You're less stressed and more juiced. Less obligated and more devoted. You get more done. When it's easy for you, you can be of greater service to the people around you.

PROCRASTINATION CAN BE DIVINE

Procrastinating is easy, and that's a fact. And even type-A personalities and productive grown-ups put things off. But what we might critique as *procrastination* can actually be a misdiagnosis for *instinct*.

One of the effects of living in a hyperproductive society is that intuitive resistance can get labeled as procrastination. But what seems like avoidance may be a deeper inkling of wrong timing.

Hesitation can be a form of wisdom. Motives become clearer; new information shows up. Amazing grace can happen when you choose inner rhythms over external pressure.

ENTHUSIASM SAVES LIVES

You know what's easy? Dreaming. Hanging out with people who make you feel good. Laughing. Resting. Being passionate.

There is nothing as easy as being inspired ■

Sometimes you have to shovel horse apples to make your dreams come true. But, ultimately, no dream will serve you if you're forcing yourself to make it happen.

Enthusiasm is a fantastic indicator of where your true strength lives. It's the immediate "I love it!" response, the game you've got to get into, the cause you can't walk away from, the idea that makes you pause and then nod, "Oh, this is a good one, a really good one." Enthusiasm evokes a determined "no matter what-ness." It wakes us up in the middle of the night with fresh ideas. Enthusiasm creates a flurry of connections and marvelous events that often starts with this powerful little phrase: "What if . . ."

Enthusiasm is a heightened state of consciousness, and it's one of the best feelings there is to feel.

Whenever there is enthusiasm, there is a creative empowerment that goes far beyond what a mere person is capable of.

—Eckhart Tolle, *A New Earth*

The word *enthusiasm* comes from the Greek root *entheos,* "having the god within." Eckhart Tolle suggests that enthusiasm is the highest form of "awakened doing."

Eckhart outlines three modalities of awakened doing: acceptance, enjoyment, and enthusiasm. *Acceptance* means being in the situation and doing what must be done willingly. *Enjoyment* happens when you are fully present and not just doing what you're doing as a means to an end. It's not what you do, but how you do it. *Enthusiasm* means that there is a deep enjoyment in what you do, plus a goal or a vision you're working toward. Enthusiasm knows where it's going.

Is that not cosmic fabulousness? So elegant and simple. So obviously essential to whole living.

Of course, you can't be in a continual state of enthusiasm. You'd fry, fall, and lose your grounding. But before you commit, sign, take the stage, take the meeting, take the gig, or take your place in the intentional unfolding of your life, enthusiasm must be present. Ideally. And we're going for ideal here.

My great friend Marie Forleo, founder of the Rich Happy & Hot LIVE events, has her own kind of enthusiasm policy for how she chooses her projects: if it isn't a "Hell yes!," then it's a no. Enthusiasm is the genuine *Yes!* that will uncork your genius, signal your muses to come down, and magnetize the resources you need to be within your reach. Enthusiasm is the beautiful beginning that changes everything.

HAVE BRIGHT FAITH

Buddhists have a term for a particular kind of enthusiasm that happens with new ideas and events: *bright faith.* This is not the bedrock kind of faith that grounds your psychology, spirituality, or devotion. It's not the assurance/insurance kind of faith where we hope/trust that life will come through for us.

It's the *Holy cow, I'm standing at the beginning of something that is so insanely ripe with potential that I wanna get naked and roll all over it right now while singing rock opera* . . . kind of faith. It makes you grin silly grins and do uncharacteristically impulsive and obsessive things. Bright faith is exhilarated.

Buddhist teacher Sharon Salzberg says, "This is a state of love-filled delight in possibilities and eager joy at the prospect of actualizing them. Bright faith goes beyond merely claiming that possibility for oneself to immersing oneself in it. . . . The enthusiasm, energy, and courage we need in order to leave the safe path, to stop aligning ourselves with the familiar and convenient, arise with bright faith."

Bright faith is primal to creativity. Bright faith is essential to falling in love—with people, with causes, with your own perfectly perfect self. Bright faith can be unnerving, slightly embarrassing, and awkward. We are trained to resist it, and we do so at the cost of innovation and the passion we crave.

THE CLARITY THAT CRAZY BRINGS

Here's a headline for a life résumé: "Selectively but wildly excitable." I adore exclusively stoked people. They're discerning—not everything is a great opportunity; in fact, golden ops are rare. But when they see something that glimmers with uniqueness or resonates with their reason for being, they start to move.

This is how brainstorming goes with brightly faithful people: "Hmmm. Uh-huh. Nope. Nah. No. Nope. Nope. Nope. Nope. Ooh. Ahh. Wait a second. Holy shit, yes, yes, yes, oh my God, we could . . . and then we could . . . and it would be so . . . and holy yes and . . . I'll sell it all if I have to . . . and what am I going to wear when I accept the award?! Who will we invite to the wedding?! How big do you think we can build it? Excuse me while I make a phone call."

They go *off*.

It's illogical, grandiose, crazy, and most certainly romantic. It's *faith*. But these are the essential ingredients for breaking through mediocrity and cynicism. Bright faith is a divine kind of madness and it feels so good if we don't judge it. And what the über-realists of the world don't quite get is that the chaotic sparks of bright faith actually burn a path to clarity of mind.

To create things of beauty—in form or between two people—is a passion-first, discrimination-second formula. And yep, it's dangerous.

COOL IS DULL

If I have to choose between two service providers with similar skill and equal pricing, I'll always go with the one who freely expresses his or her excitement. I did a gig with someone who said, "Oh, my God, I'm so excited to work with you! I'm going to hang up the phone and do the happy dance." She was so uncool about it all. No pretense—just joy and bright faith in how much fun we could have. So then I said, "Me, too! Now I'm really stoked. I'll do the happy dance when I hang up, too. Let's *do* this!"

My best strategic meetings have been the most uncool. Whether they're construction contractors, publishers, or florists, they're unself-conscious and eager. They're stoked to be there and they say so.

Bright faith shows up at the beginning—that extremely precious and fractional space when you need as much light as you can to see which way you want to go. The more possibilities you let shine—the more *you* shine with possibility—the more lucid and discerning you can be. It's that easy.

EASY PRIORITIES

WORKSHEET

1. **What actually needs to get done in your life and livelihood?** As in, *must happen* in order for things to basically run smoothly.

2. **What's your competency level for each activity?** Lame, sufficient, great, brilliant? (This is not about whether or not you enjoy it, or whether you need to be the one to execute it.)

3. Out of your list of "needs to get done," **which of those activities actually makes you feel strengthened,** vitalized, and more alive when you do them?

4. Out of the list of "needs to get done," **which of those activities doesn't really light your fire,** or outright annoy you?

5. Open your heart and mind when you scan your list. You may not be stellar at an activity, but it could feel really inspiring when you do it. And you might think that an activity is perhaps "beneath" you, yet you feel strengthened when you do it. **What can you do to develop these strengths and interests?** Coaching, classes, courses, training, attending events, reading books, connecting with people, pursuing mentors, setting aside sacred time?

6. What three actions will you take *this week* to condition and **nourish your true strengths?**

7. What three actions will you take *this week* to **decrease your time** spent on the activities that drag you down and don't feed your true strengths?

longing wishing

crave aspire

wanting choosing

more

desire

SESSION 3

the
strategy
of desire

The longing for happiness and freedom from suffering
expresses the great natural potential of mind.

—Dzigar Kongtrul Rinpoche, Tibetan Buddhist lama

This could be the single most important takeaway from this book.
Here it is:

How do you want to feel? ■

How do you want to feel when you look at your schedule for the week? When you get dressed in the morning? When you walk through the door of your studio or your office? When you pick up the phone? When you cash the check, accept the award, finish your masterpiece, make the sale, or fall in love? . . .

How do you want to feel?

Knowing how you actually want to feel is the most potent form of clarity that you can have.

Generating those feelings is the most creative thing you can do with your life ■

You've got a to-do list, right? Quarterly objectives? Raise your hand if you set yearly goals. Five-year goals? Now, who has a list of how they want to feel in their life? Whenever I ask this question to audiences, only a few hands sprout up from the crowd. (A few more if we're on the West Coast.)

We have the procedures of achievement upside down. We set our sights on the babe, the boat, the bucks. We get them. Sometimes. They make us happy. Sometimes. We set a goal, we reach it, we feel great. Unless, of course, we feel empty or flustered or anxious that what we're doing isn't working to fill the hole in our soul.

Let me say it another way: Typically we come up with our to-do lists, our bucket lists, and our strategic plans—all the stuff we want to have, get, and experience outside of ourselves. All of those aspirations are being driven by an innate desire to feel a certain way. What if, first, we got clear on how we actually wanted to feel within ourselves, and *then* we designed our to-do lists?

Maybe what you want to feel is "energized" or "joyful." For years, you've been thinking you want a three-thousand-square-foot house in the city and to be promoted to VP. You *should* want a bigger house and a bigger job, right? Bigger is growth, right?

But maybe those things aren't energizing or joy inducing at all. You could be mortgage poor and working sixty hours a week. Perhaps energizing and joyful would come from a stylin' little condo, and you could use your extra money to see one European city a year and help put your nephew through school. And maybe you don't need the ego-stroking title or the extra few grand a year from being promoted. Perhaps staying where you are with work and taking a new course outside of the job—or doing a work exchange—would be infinitely more energizing and joyful.

And not everyone needs to feel all wild 'n' wind-in-her-hair. Stable, comfortable, safe, financially secure—this same theory applies as much to grounded sensibilities as it does to the audacious. Your core desired feelings don't have to be radical . . . you just have to know what they are so you can go about making them a reality.

When you're clear on how you want to feel, your decision making gets to the heart of the matter.

Sometimes when you reach a milestone, you discover that achievement is not always what it appeared to be from afar. We need to scrutinize those "logical next steps"—like living together and getting married because it's the obvious thing to do. Or working your way up the ladder. Or accumulating more stuff.

How do you know that you're working toward a goal that will be truly satisfying when you achieve it? You can't. It's impossible to predict. But it is possible to stack the odds of fulfillment in your favor, because it's not really about the babe, the boat, or the bucks. It's about the feeling that you're going after.

First, get clear on how you want to feel.

Then, do stuff that makes you feel that way.

Without exception, everything on our to-do, to-get, to-experience lists originates in the feelings we desire. You eat what you eat, make what you make, hang with the people you hang with, say what you say because you believe that those actions are going to create a favorable reaction inside of you. We do stuff to feel good.

Even when we do stuff that's "bad" for us (eating glazed doughnuts when we're on a diet, overspending when we're on a budget), we're still feeding that part of our psyche that says, "Right now, doing X will make me feel Y. And Y will make me feel good, better, relieved, safe, alive . . . " The doughnut feels good going down. The mistakes seem like the best decisions at the time.

Feelings are magnetic.

You can call it the power of positive thinking, a self-fulfilling prophecy, or the law of attraction. Attitude is driven by emotion and emotions are beacons. Gratitude creates more reasons to be grateful. **Generosity creates a generous response.** Power evokes strength. What we focus on expands. So choosing to focus on the feelings that you want to feel is a surer way to create the experience that you want to experience.

WANT WHAT YOU WANT

Knowing how you want to feel is half the journey to liberation. But a funny thing often happens on the way to clarity. We get clear on how we want to feel, and then we muck it all up with self-judgment. A story:

I was jamming with a client whom I adore. She's kindhearted, she's willing to look at her shit and her gloriousness, and she's excellent at what she does.

"So in terms of 'success' how do you want to feel?" I asked her.

"I . . . I want to feel important," she said, like it was confession time. And then it came, the backpedal, the squashing of desire: "But is it wrong to want to feel that way? It sounds a bit arrogant. Shouldn't I want to feel something else?"

Freeze frame. It's not wrong to want to feel a certain way. You want what you want. It doesn't mean you'll get it, but denying it won't get you anywhere better.

Back to the convo:

"Is it wrong to want to feel important?" I echoed back to her. "Well, maybe some therapists would think so. Could be your wounded inner child 'n' all that, but let's work from here and now. In terms of your business, what would make you feel important?"

"Well, that actress I was telling you about would be photographed in my product. And the editor at that big magazine would decide to put me on the cover for the next issue. I'd be seated at the head table of the industry gala. My cheap clients would stop pestering me for cheaper product, and I would be working with the people who really value what I do." She was on a roll. Her voice was clear and strong. She was sitting up straight.

"Uh-huh. Well, that sounds like a rocking business to me. So, what do you need to do to help ensure that you feel important?" I asked. And with that, a very concise to-do list rolled off her lips. Bang, bang, bang. She knew exactly what to do.

"You know, just talking about what I'm going to do to make myself feel important makes me feel . . . important," she concluded.

That's what happens when we take control of our desires. Moving toward gratitude helps you feel grateful. Aiming for power gets your power circuits firing. Planning for love makes you feel lovable. And so it goes.

Be done with feeling guilty for wanting to feel the way you want to feel. Follow your desired emotion. Don't analyze it too deeply. Just let it roll and rumble a bit. It may be there to humble you, expand you, heal, surprise, or reinvent you. Anywhere it leads, it's there for a divine reason.

FEELINGS + TIME MANAGEMENT

If you have goal lists or vision boards, write your desired feelings on them—front and center. Stick a note of your key feelings into your daily planner.

I have a sticky note inside my Moleskine planner that says CON-NECTED. AFFLUENT. DIVINELY FEMININE. INNOVATIVE.

And that teeny note, those few words, are the rudder of my ship. David Allen, the king of prioritization and time management, gives the most refreshing answer to the question "How do you set priorities?"

"I have a radical point of view: Learn to listen to, and trust, your heart. Or your intuition, or your gut, or the seat of your pants, or whatever part of your anatomy is the source of that mysteriously wonderful 'still, small voice' that somehow knows you better than you do, and knows what's better for you, better than you do."

Letting your feelings be your time management guide? Radical indeed.

Open heart, open mind.

When you're rooted to your desired feelings, it feels safer to open your heart. You become more focused on how new situations make you feel, rather than how they appear on the surface.

Let's say that a business project comes your way. You immediately click with the people involved—you feel a great sense of harmony. When you imagine working on the project, you feel enthusiastic, creative, and useful—all of the things you most want to feel in your life. But! The project doesn't "look" like you thought your ideal job would. It's in an industry you never expected to be working in. Normally, you'd immediately say: "Sorry, I don't work in textiles or with food companies; I'm focused on the kids and the nonprofit sector."

But you can't deny the good feelings that the project elicits. You feel good. You say yes. You expand.

This theory also applies to love. You always pictured your true love as tall, with a healthy savings account, but the one who makes you laugh your ass off and feel more alive is short on inches and a few bucks. Feelings don't lie.

"Feelings first" is really the essence of simplified living—a focus on what matters most.

PRACTICALLY INFLUENTIAL

So this is how it works: **What can you do today, as in right now, to feel the way you want to feel?** Generating your core desired feelings doesn't just happen with affirmations you stick on your bathroom mirror, or from sitting in the lotus position and *om*-ing your way into an altered state. Mindfulness and contemplation is only half of the equation. You've got to take some action, Jackson.

Small things, incremental things, tiny gestures: anything to counter the glums or the clench of despair. Do it. Daring, grand, big, dramatic, life-affirming actions. Whatever positively generates the feelings you long for and moves your life forward. Take baby steps or go quantum. **Stay focused on your feelings.**

One of my core desired feelings is *affluence*. For me, affluence is about abundance and flow. I long for flowing ideas and creativity. It's about having influence in the lives of the people I can touch—whether that's a smile to let them know that they are seen and loved, or an insight that I can offer. Affluence is about thriving, from phat cash flow to an unceasing spirit of generosity. It's electric and prosperous and lavish. I don't need to fit the typical über-wealthy or "comes from money" definitions of affluent (too late for that anyway—I hail from a factory town). I rock *my* version of affluence. And it feels amazing.

But not always, of course. Some days I'm scrambling to attain, achieve, have. And I lose sight for a minute of how rich I am in love, health, awareness, and Western world privileges. So I do what I need to do that day to create the sensation of affluent. That includes simple, easy-to-do gestures. I can retweet someone's blog post and send some Web traffic their way; make my monthly donation to Women for Women International a week earlier than planned; get dressed up for errands; buy a sandwich for the homeless guy on the corner; send a thank-you note or two; or go visit the Jacobsen chair that I'm hankering for—just sitting in that chair makes me feel all quality 'n' sass. I can make a special trip to the Italian deli just for a small package of goat cheese that comes with an edible flower on top of it—dairy luxe. I can read an old love letter. I can take two minutes to thank God for absolutely everything.

For a moment I feel somewhat lacking, and then I'm back in the groove of how I really want to feel. And I start making different choices . . . that lead to greater experiences of . . . affluence.

You want to feel your core desired feelings no matter what's going on around you. Bright, no matter what the weather; confident, no matter how hard the knocks; affluent, no matter how skinny your bank account is.

When you feel, say, affluent, you act, think, and radiate affluence. Your mind expands to accommodate affluent thoughts and strategies. With the pleasing sensation of affluence in your heart—from the simple act of making a phone call to help someone get a job, to asking for a better interest rate—you will tap into more ideas and strategies that are aligned with the energy of affluence. Most simply put: **When you feel good, you act smarter.**

If you act out in anger, things usually don't go so well. Negative feelings = dark results. What if you act out in harmony or vitality? Or if you let feeling beautiful or connected get the better of you? Positive feelings = brighter actions = brilliant results.

DECONSTRUCTING SUCCESS

In the worksheet at the end of this session, you will be asked to write out how you want to feel, and then you'll be guided to narrow down those feelings more specifically. It's really a cool exercise.

Life is full of opportunities to feel exactly the way you want to feel ■

But, before you go there, we need to talk about success.

As a term, *success* is up there with *nice* and *plastic*—it covers just about everything but doesn't tell you much at all.

Even the dictionary definition of success is weak:

SUC·CESS *(NOUN)*

1. the favorable or prosperous termination of attempts or endeavors
2. the attainment of wealth, position, honors, or the like
3. a successful performance or achievement
4. a person or thing that is successful

Whatever it is, we all want it, and we want it bad. But (here I go again), what does success actually feel like? What does it sound like, smell like, look like, and taste like? Contrary to what the progenitors and propagators of the (North) American Dream would tell you, success is actually a very personal thing.

You're allowed to desire any feeling you want, of course. But for the purposes of this exercise, I'm suggesting that you do yourself a favor and strike the word *success* from your vocabulary. Beneath *successful* are likely more poignant emotions that you desire. Dig deeper.

CORE DESIRED FEELINGS

W O R K S H E E T

feelings: sensations; emotions; inner states; consciousness; inner world

goal: everything you work toward; the objective of your strategy; the whole point

FEELING

How do you want to feel in your life?

Do a stream-of-consciousness riff: concepts, words, feelings, images. This is about optimal, positive, nourishing, and good—very good—feelings. Put them all on paper. Let a tsunami of desire flood you. Invest in yourself. Want what you want. Go.

PATTERN RECOGNITION

Study your list of desired feelings. Read it over a few times. Read it out loud if you're inclined. Sleep on it. Take it for a walk. What jumps out at you, feels warm, feels *yes!,* feels really important and valuable? Identify the words or concepts that really turn you on.

The objective of this exercise is to narrow down your list to three to five desired feelings. Whittle it down; make some tough choices. Having a tough time choosing between, say, *creative* and *artistic,* or *strong* and *powerful*? Try this: Look up the definitions of words. Each word is its own planet, and knowing the actual definition and origin can be instantly illuminating.

continues on next page

Repetitive questioning. This is a potentially annoying, galvanizing little mind trick: Keep asking yourself how a feeling feels. Get underneath its skin. Like this:

So, what does *confidence* feel like?
(Answer with the first thing that comes to mind.)
"It feels like winning."

What does *confidence* feel like?
"It feels like being certain."

What does *confidence* feel like?
"It feels like . . . clarity."

Bingo. What you really desire to feel is clarity.

Write each word you're considering on its own sticky note, even if it's ten words. Stick them on the fridge for a day, or around your computer monitor, and see how they make you feel. You'll start to see how *confidence* is really summed up with the word *strong,* or how *beautiful, classy,* and *elegant* are present in one word: *graceful*. Toss the sticky notes that don't make the cut and see what you're left with after a few days.

Set a deadline for yourself. "By Saturday, I'll be clear on my core desired feelings and that's that." Don't sweat it. This isn't a test. You can change your mind later, have an aha moment, and recalibrate it all when you wake up.

ACT THE WAY YOU WANT TO FEEL

Five to ten accomplishments or experiences that will make me feel this way:

Three things I will do today to generate these feelings:

Three things I will do this week to generate these feelings:

Three things I will do this quarter to generate these feelings:

Three people to collaborate with who help me feel this way:

part2

questions

inquiring asking

seeking

answers

open doors

questions

inquiring asking

seeking answers

open doors

SESSION 4

the
burning
questions

The one who asks
questions doesn't lose his way.

—African proverb

When we have arrived at the question, the answer is already near.

—Ralph Waldo Emerson

Often just asking a question put changes in motion. Even if you don't have the answer, a good question stirs up reality. This is why the master poet Rilke implores us to "Live the questions themselves, live them now!" That starts with asking more questions of one another and ourselves. Ceaselessly.

1. WHEN SOMEONE AT A PARTY ASKS YOU WHAT YOU DO, WHAT DO YOU SAY? AND HOW DO YOU *FEEL* WHEN YOU SAY IT?

The "So, what do you do?" question makes a lot of us look for the exit sign. I've worked with CEOs and MBAs who just dread it. Stay-at-home parents with law degrees particularly loathe this question. Like Charlie: "When asked this question, I usually stumble around and say that I am a lawyer, but not practicing. And that I've been writing. I haven't felt comfortable saying that I am a writer because until relatively recently, I hadn't sold a book. I usually toss in there that I am taking care of my two young kids. When I say these things, I feel clumsy and insecure. I know that I mention the law thing first because it is the most quintessentially important thing

I have done. When I answer this question, I feel a bit scattered, pulled in different directions, which is something I feel very often." Just takes one benign question asked innocently by a stranger to unravel all your issues, doesn't it?

Big-cash consultants who'd rather be working on a hobby farm or writing a mystery novel rile against this question, because when they answer, they feel like fat fakers. Faking pride is a special kind of painful.

Other people are bursting with enthusiasm to share what they do. Or calm with confidence in the place that they've carved out in the world. These people have a twinkle to them. Even the tired ones shimmer.

It doesn't matter if you're a VP or a hospice volunteer, a trust fund baby or a perpetual student, you need to have a genuine cocktail line, an elevator pitch, a clear one-liner about what you do in the world. Note: *genuine*. Not the chips of truth that put the "small" in small talk.

Why do you need a genuine cocktail line? You could be riding the elevator with your next future customer, lover, funder, best friend, or a primetime TV producer. When serendipitous promotion and soul sparks fly, it's good to be on your mark.

But mostly, it's a practice in presence. How you introduce yourself could be a sacred distillation of your reality, talent, and deepest interest. Yep—all that in just a sentence or two. Clearly, this is no trivial exercise.

It's better for your nervous system if your description of your current career or life status feels honest to you when you deliver it. Let me clarify: It doesn't mean that you have to feel stupendous about what you're doing to make your money. If you hate your day job, then you hate your day job. It means you feel the freedom of being genuine about where you're at.

BURNING ANSWERS
When someone asks what I do . . .

"I feel confident, proud, excited."

"I secretly enjoy that most people haven't the slightest idea what my day-to-day work looks like."

"I usually say I work for the city, but then follow it up with the fact that pottery is my passion, and my goal is to leave the city and do pottery full time."

"I feel like I have to qualify what I'm doing to convey the fact that I feel I'm under-achieving."

"I feel yucky—like I'm letting myself down."

"I know that I'm in the right profession, which is a blessing every day."

"I feel like a rock star."

Let's say that you're plotting to get off payroll, and that you're at legal and political liberty to publicly express yourself—you're not going to get fired or crash your company's stock price if word gets out that your nine-to-five gig blows. Take Kirk, for example, a guy I met at one of those brainwashing personal development weekends where they let you out only once a day to pee. Kirk felt that pouring cement five days a week was not moving him up on the social food chain. He was literally slogging through. But he told it straight, without being a downer, and he painted a picture of his bigger self: "What do I do? I dig ditches to pay the bills right now. But what I'm really stoked about is the night class I'm taking in import/export law. I also volunteer at the Westside Youth Shelter a few times a month." Kirk showed up as a whole person and got instant respect.

What if you're one of the many who feel purposeless and lost at sea? How do you turn that into an impressive opening? First, **forget about being impressive and commit to being real.** I met Erica at a talk I gave in Dallas to a group of bighearted, highly accessorized power *chicas*. "What do I do? I'm a talent recruiter by day and Kundalini yoga teacher by night. Someday I'll stop living a double life, but right now, I'm, you know, digging for my dream gig. Mostly, I'm interested in wellness and modern art." No complaining. Sincerely searching. Impressive.

ACCENTUATE YOUR INTERESTS

Your interests are where your true strengths—and the truly magical connections—come to life. Your interests or so-called hobbies are just as relevant as your income-earning status and how many stamps your passport has. People who are **interested in life** are the most interesting people. Interest and presence tops worldly any day.

GIVE YOURSELF CREDIT

I did some business and marketing strategy with a woman who introduced herself simply as "an athletic coach." I figured she was a freelance coach with a few local clients. It turned out that she actually had a crew of coaches working under her that she had trained in her own licensable methodology. She had a thriving team and company that worked with high-performance athletes from all over the world. She was not *just* "an athletic coach."

"Okay, let me be you for a minute. I'm going to just state the facts," I told her, about to do some branding kung fu on her empire. "I have an athletic performance company called Power Racing. My coaching team and I design training programs for athletes . . . mostly Ironman competitors, but we do take on other types of cross athletes—and from anywhere in the world, actually. It's part science, part motivation." Done.

"Wow, I sound great!" she said. "And, it's all true!"

Let people see the full scope of what you're doing. You can be modest *and* powerful. Factual *and* engaging. Facts + feelings = genuinely compelling.

FEELINGS OVER FACTS

My Swiss friend—aka Bruno Zee Hot Swiss Man—tells me that it's considered rude in his homeland to ask someone what they do "for a living" as soon as you meet them. "Too forward," he says. "How do you say in English? '*It's tacky.*'" I don't entirely agree, but I appreciate the romance of a more circuitous approach. Eventually, we all get around to wondering what someone does for a living.

The problem with introducing a conversation with this question is that the answer can shut down a more meaningful exchange. We're prone to put people in categories according to their jobs: winner, loser, somewhat intriguing, or totally unrelatable.

There's a quick, sure fix for this dilemma. The question: "How does it feel to . . . ?"

I scored a last-minute ticket to a Broadway show and during intermission got to chatting with my seat neighbor. She talked about having come with a school bus of kids, who were tucked off in the balcony. "Are you a teacher?" I guessed.

"I'm the school principal. We drive up from Philly once a year to bring the theater kids to a show. They love it." We chatted about the thrill of live theater and New York City.

"So how does it feel to be the school principal?" I circled back to her.

She stopped, lifted her eyebrows in soft surprise, and shook her head. "Hmmm. I've been doing this for fifteen years and I don't think anyone has ever asked me how I felt about it." We both smiled quietly, nodding in recognition. I stayed quiet. "It's still a privilege," she replied, straightening up her neck scarf. "I still feel . . . honored."

We weren't strangers anymore.

2. WHAT DO PEOPLE THANK YOU FOR MOST OFTEN? WHAT DO THEY COME TO YOU FOR, OR SAY ABOUT YOU, MOST FREQUENTLY ("POSITIVE" OR "NEGATIVE")?

Create a habit of noticing where and when appreciation comes to you in your life and work. Is it always in a particular realm? For example, caretaking, solution finding, listening, creative thinking, beauty making? Gratitude is a feedback loop that will show you where you are thriving.

The gratitude you receive from others is a reflection of your genius ■

BURNING ANSWERS

I feel powerful when . . .

"I look hot." **"When I'm talking about something that I know a lot about."** "When I'm clear and rooted in a place of clarity—there's a balance between heart and intellect, spirit and form." **"I feel really awesome at getting things started."** "When I'm writing a piece of work that I know is supposed to be born." **"Making love."** "Making a space beautiful." **"When I'm willing to walk away from a deal."** "Swimming." **"I feel on fire when I am dancing—and it makes me feel like nothing else."** "I get really excited (but terrified) when I'm performing on stage." **"When I'm paying for my son's first year of school, it feels like I'm doing the right thing."** "After I make a green smoothie." **"I feel useful when I can lead a team or a discussion."** "I used to train volunteers to counsel survivors of sexual assault, and those weekends made me feel so incredibly useful and helpful." **"Planning trips or ideas or events."** "There are times in my life where I've just been 'in the flow,' and it seemed like everything I did was exactly the right thing." **"It's that place where everyday life thrills me to the core. I can get there by filling up my time with the things that I love doing and the people who I love."**

3. WHEN DO YOU FEEL POWERFUL, PASSIONATE, FREE, INCREDIBLY USEFUL, EXCITED, INSPIRED?

You want to live and earn from this zone, right? Please say yes. When you're in this passion zone, you lose track of time or you'd work for free. It might make your body feel stronger; it makes you feel energized.

4. WHAT DO YOU THINK YOUR FORM OF GENIUS IS? WHAT ARE YOU AMAZING AT (WORK OR LIFE RELATED)?

Genius is the ability to receive
from the universe.

—*I Ching*

It always breaks my heart a little when someone doesn't think that they're amazing at anything in particular. It pulls on every maternal impulse I have and I want to get all Dolly Parton and say, *But God don't make junk, sugar pie! God done gave everyone a gift, a coat of many colors, baby!*

If you're in that gray zone, wondering what could possibly be exceptional about you, then the best place to begin is by investigating what turns you on in your everyday and fantasy life. It's in those places that you'll start to see your own insight emerge. Can you think of a better assignment?

5. WHO DO YOU THINK IS REALLY COOL OR ELEGANT OR POWERFUL?

I can't tell you how many people answer "Angelina Jolie" to this question. I mentioned this fact to an audience of Mormon mompreneurs in Salt Lake City and they gasped. So I guess "Amazonian Hollywood UN Goddess Sexpot Supermom" isn't what we all aspire to.

Your aspirations show up in your admiration. Mother Teresa's mystical devotion, Obama's steady character, Angelina's boldness, your grandparents' integrity—all qualities that are latent or burgeoning within you. You are what you're attracted to, so it's mighty useful to ask yourself why you dig who you dig. In Session 11 we'll get into this more with an exercise on people who influence you.

6. WHAT'S CHRONIC, REPETITIVE, OR INFLAMED IN YOUR INNER OR OUTER LIFE?

Muscles get inflamed and choked from repetitive overuse. And it takes just one overtaxed muscle to stifle an entire limb, which then throws off the alignment of our whole body. When we stop using the muscle in the same way, blood flow can return and pain makes way for vitality. In the same way, an old

BURNING ANSWERS

I'm genius because . . .

"I can inspire others to take action when no one else can." **"I'm an excellent systems creator."** "I'm deeply insightful. I can see problems in a few seconds and something in me can quickly draw a path to the solution." **"I'm the best gift giver, ever. I always know what someone will love."** "I'm a fabulous, loving mother." **"I can tear up the dance floor."** "I'm able to break down an extremely complicated process so pretty much anyone can do it." **"My form of genius is using my intuition with most everything I do."** "I am the choreographer of awesome customer service." **"When I am in process with someone or a group I am 'on' and am guided to move and speak to the context in front of me."** "My system senses and then I make choices based on this intuition." **"I could sell ice to an Eskimo."** "I 'see' blocks of energy as form and density." **"I never hold back."** "I feel the energy within and in the field around someone and act accordingly." **"I meet people right where they are and coach them into breakthrough terrain."** "I can tell stories that make big (even overwhelmingly big) issues relevant to people."

psychic wound or one small behavior continually repeated could strain our whole life. **Freedom starts when you can identify the aggravation you've been accommodating for so long.**

Rory was one of those big thinkers with the best of intentions. Lots of friends. Plenty of ideas. Sweet soul that she is, she couldn't get a project off the ground to save her life. Nothing took hold long enough to show a profit or get results. She was so pushy that funders or advisers would back away. She would start out all gung ho and then drop everything because she felt called to get away from it all. A flight attendant friend offered her a free seat to India, so she put her campaign of the month on hold and headed off. She'd fall for a guy who was an inventor or whose cousin was an Internet marketer, and get pumped on the promise of their business. Their shiny new thing then became her shiny new thing.

Rory and I were talking about earning money and I slipped this question in: "So, where in your life do things feel inflamed, or monotonously irritating for you?"

Her answer was quick, which made it clear that she was on an obsessive loop about it. "What still burns my ass is that I've been trying, to no avail, to forgive my father for cutting me out of the will. I think about it every week." In the context of our discussion about money hang-ups, a light switched on for her and that *holy duh* look came over her face. "And guess what?! I'm always inclined to go get a loan or a freebie instead of just going to earn more of my own money. I'm still trying to get something that's supposedly owed to me." Sisters doin' it for themselves, heard on high.

Whatever thorn you might have in your side could be affecting the way you go about everything. Locate it.

BURNING ANSWERS

My chronic condition is . . .

"I have a repetitive martyr syndrome that is getting real old." **"There's an odd pattern of my getting into wrangles with customer service people. Their 'dumb' behavior hooks my sense of entitlement and superiority."** "My perfectionist tendencies (or at least that's what I've labeled them) keep me from pulling the trigger." **"Smallness."** "Self-doubt." **"Not believing I am allowed to."** "Comparing myself to others." **"Not believing I 'can.'"** "Being competitive."

7. WHAT'S ALWAYS IN THE BACK OF YOUR MIND?

You are what you think about all day.

—Allen Ginsberg

Thoughts have flavor. There is a subtle and important distinction between what is inflamed in your psyche and what dwells in the background of it. Here we're trying to hone in on the thoughts and feelings that have a floating or amorphous quality to them—more like a cloud than a thorn. These thought forms can feel ominous or delightful, or both. But they're not screaming at you. More likely, they're speaking softly and steadily and they're pleased when you pay attention to them.

8. WHAT WOULD YOU LIKE TO STOP DOING?

When someone has the good sense and conviction to stop doing what's not working for them, well, it calls for a national holiday. The brilliance of simplification needs to be celebrated!

It often goes like this:

I'm going to *stop*: "Being stingy with myself." **"Worrying what others will think of me and just *go for it*."** "Worrying that I will be called out as a fraud. (I have classic impostor syndrome.)" **"Worrying so much."** "Worrying that other people are mad at me." **"I'd like to stop being so fucking self-conscious."** "Working with that client—every time I see her name in my in-box, I get a sick feeling in my stomach." **"Cleaning my kids' rooms for them."** "Planning every date with my man when, really, I want him to plan our dates." **"Undercharging, underearning, underselling myself."**

"Being the administrator. The money isn't worth it." **"Doing everything myself."**

In Session 9, you'll find "The Stop-Doing List." Prepare for ecstatic liberation.

9. HOW MUCH MONEY WOULD YOU *LIKE* TO BE MAKING?

Note: Heiresses and tycoons may be excused from this exercise. And possibly students. And anyone with money socked away. Oh, and forest dwellers living off the grid.

It doesn't matter what you do for a living or from where your money flows; declaring how much money you want to earn, attract, and throw down is mighty empowering.

What you're targeting is a number that would make you feel really happy. We want to avoid lurking fears of being a bag lady and zero-to-mogul delusions of grandeur. Sugar mama and lottery fantasies need to be parked.

If your income declaration has a flavor of rebellion or feverishness to it, you might want to rein it in a bit. "I wanna rake in a million bucks this year!" (Says dude who just launched his first blog and has $75K in credit card debt.) The desire has to come from a peaceful place. I'm not saying don't aim high—quantum leaps and breakthroughs happen all of the time. Point to where you'd feel proud and fulfilled. Ultimately, this is about creating wellness, not gluttony or exhaustion. Run a few numbers through your mind that make you grin and think, "Yeah, with some tight strategy and a big scoop of magic, that could actually happen this year." Aim for that.

MASCULINE MONEY

Interesting factoid: Men tend to answer this money question with predictable specificity. They name dollar figures, they list off each revenue stream, they put it all in order of profitability. That kind of awareness and openness is very effective. **What gets measured gets attention. What gets attention grows.**

DECLARING HOW MUCH MONEY YOU'D LIKE TO EARN . . .

Gives you a goal, for Chrissakes. This may sound oversimplified, but when you know what you really want to make in a year, you can do what it takes to . . . go make it. You can break it down. You can target. You want to make $150K? Great. How many units do you need to ship? What project will put you on the map for a raise? How many clients do you need to service? What does your profit margin need to be?

What if you have a set or salaried income? Do *not* let that hem in your earning desires. There are raises, bonuses, promotions, discounts, new jobs, surprise opportunities, wealthy new lovers, generous gifts, free piles, air miles, aunties who will leave you their land, and investments that soar. Make. The. Declaration.

Puts it into perspective—and fast. You may add up your financial goals with the time you work in a month and realize that you're really making zilch per hour. Or you might determine that, in actuality, you don't need to have a mil in the bank and two cars in the family to live a rich life. When you know where you stand, your aim can be more direct.

Makes you feel capable, and when you feel capable, you act capable. With your **desire declared,** you'll start to see ways of making things happen. When you lock on to a material goal, you unlock your capacities to manifest. You'll see potential collaborators more clearly. Dormant and fresh ideas will rise to the surface. You'll make connections between players and strategies.

Sets you up for playtime and rewards. When you start to close in on your money goal, you can plan to party. Plan a holiday, revel in the peace, let a healthy sense of pride soothe your ambitious bones.

Sends a message to your subconscious, and your subconscious takes things very literally. (This is one of those times when you *want* your subconscious to take you literally.)

Sends a signal to your tribe that you're in it to win it. The people who love and respect you—friends, coaches, mentors, partners—will not only hold you accountable to your goals, they'll likely do whatever they can to help you get to where you want to go. Throw a party for all of them when you get there.

10. HOW WOULD YOU LIKE TO BE SEEN, RECOGNIZED, ACKNOWLEDGED, AWARDED, PRAISED?

Do you want to win an Academy Award or just have your acting coach tell you that your performance moved him to tears? What would motivate you more: a pay raise, or having your boss tell the team that she just couldn't do it without you? Do you need a love poem written just for you, or just to have your partner get up and greet you when you walk in the door? Some of us want to be preeminent in our field. Some of us just want the person who matters most to us to tell us that they need us.

11. SO . . . WHAT WOULD YOU LIKE TO DO WITH YOUR LIFE AND CAREER? MONEY IS NO OBJECT. DREAM.

Session 6, "Visioneering," revolves around this question. Now's a good time to get your dream on.

THE BURNING QUESTIONS

W O R K S H E E T

1. When someone at a party asks you what you do, what do you say? And how do you *feel* when you say it?

2. What do people thank you for most often? What do they come to you for, or say about you, most frequently (positive or negative)?

3. When do you feel powerful, passionate, free, incredibly useful, excited, inspired?

4. What do you think your form of genius is? What are you amazing at (work or life related)?

5. Who do you think is really cool or elegant or powerful?

6. What's chronic, repetitive, or inflamed in your inner or outer life?

7. What's always in the back of your mind?

8. What would you like to stop doing?

9. How much money would you *like* to be making?

10. How would you like to be seen, recognized, acknowledged, awarded, praised?

11. So . . . what would you like to do with your life and career? (Money is no object. Dream.)

essential positive

deliberate now

succinct bam shine

accessible

connected

distinguished distinct

present presence

SESSION 5

facing
forward

You can't change the world from the rearview mirror.

—Anita Roddick, founder of The Body Shop

Before we get to unfolding our most marvelous future, we need to put the past in its place. When I used to work with small Fire Starter groups, we'd go around the room and introduce ourselves to kick things off.

When you introduce yourself, please give us:

- **Your cocktail line.** Describe what you do in a sentence or two.
- **One word that might describe your "brand,"** be it personal or professional—and don't worry if nothing comes to mind, or if you're compelled to throw out some strange word like *velvet* or *electric*. Just go with it.
- **Your current career challenge.** It could be cash flow, life balance, writer's block, or staffing—whatever.
- And here's the catch: **You can't talk about your past.** It doesn't matter how many master's degrees you've earned, or how the economy walloped your sales last year. Focus on what you're doing now, on who you are today.

Here's why I try to get people focused in this way. . . . (*Warning:* instructive but unsympathetic cynicism ahead.)

When I hear an introduction that goes something like the following one, I can predict that cash flow is jammed, work-life balance is off, or something is generally way out of whack:

I'm Jane. I have a widget company that I started eleven and a half years ago (*fails to mention name of the actual company*). Shortly after I started the business, which I used all of my savings to do (*yep, that's what it takes—you won't get much sympathy from this crowd*), I got divorced (*sad, but irrelevant to the point of the conversation*). That really affected my debt load. I started with six staff and then cut back to two, and now I work more than I really want to (*your choice*). My widgets are the best on the market (*this is quite possible, but it's getting harder to believe*), but I haven't had time to get a great distributor (*you haven't made time*)—it's so hard to find good help, you know? (*If you believe it is, then it is.*) I've worked with a number of distributors but had to fire them because they didn't really believe in the product. So my challenge, I guess . . . is . . . distribution, which, of course, affects cash flow. So I guess my challenge is really cash flow.

Uh-huh.

No, sweet Jane, your challenge is that you're stuck in the past and you're chronically complaining about your present. It's a drag. **Face forward. We want to look ahead with you. Look backward, and you lose us.**

Try this, love:

I'm Jane Smith, the founder and CEO of Wild Widgets. *Industrial Magazine* named us Top Widget Maker of the Midwest, which was a huge honor in our business. I've scaled back from six to two staff and am looking to build back a really strong team so I can live more of my life. I've struggled to find really crackerjack distributors—they are critical to going from a $1-million-dollar company to my vision, which is $10 million within the next two years. So my challenge is identifying the winners—the right people to get on board. And if you need widgets, you can find us at WildWidgets.com. Thanks.

Jane! Baby! I'm so impressed with your clarity and stamina that I want to help you find a legion of supporters, right now.

Here's a guide point that will never lead you astray: Intend to shine. You can be modest about your great success; you can be honest about your fears; you can be proud and loud without the arrogance appetizer. You can be a magnet for goodness even in hard times, if you simply choose to accentuate the positive and focus on where you want to go.

Let's use a romantic analogy. We're going to ask Jack, "Jack, what's your ideal relationship look like to you?" The reason we're asking is that we're genuinely interested in other people's aspirations. And the reason Jack is compelled to share his dream with us is because he knows on some level, even if it's only in the chambers of his broken heart, that actually verbalizing what you want might help you get it. "So, Jack, what do you want the love of your life to be like?"

And then it happens. As if Jack has a learning disability because he doesn't seem to understand what you mean by "ideal" or "want," he starts talking about his ex-wife, and all the women he's dated who haven't quite fit the bill, and what a drag it is to be single. Poor guy. Jack should hook up with Jane, but they'd probably just disappoint each other.

An essential detail on the path to positivity: **You can't face forward until you've processed your past.** If your history goes unexamined and ignored, it can become an annoying character that keeps showing up in your life script—in your conversations, in your thoughts. And every time you go to make plans for the future, your past pain will enter the scene and say, "Hey, don't forget about me."

If you can assess how yesterday's agony affected you, then you not only defuse its potential grip on you, but you also place it where you want it to be in your psyche. By observing it, you transform it.

The willingness to interpret and integrate the lessons of hardship is a key characteristic to forward-facing people. They get it. And they move on.

And there is a direct correlation between forward-facing people and productive output. If I ask you, "So, tell me what would be ideal for you," and you jump in right away with vivid nouns and adjectives as if you're in the middle of your own movie, then I think to myself, "list." I can almost guarantee that just moments into our conversation you'll start to literally or mentally build a new list for making it happen. Within a week you'll be emailing me to say the new magic list is checkin', check, and *checked*. Go-getters know where they want to go, and it isn't backward.

The past is never as relevant as we think it is ■

PURGE THE PAST URGE

WORKSHEET

Failure: it sucked hard; didn't work; tanked; was rather regrettable; most definitely rough; painful; oops; bad move; agony; lost; reputation damaged; tough times; ouch.

Lesson: live and learn; made you better; much to be grateful for if you really think about it; something to laugh about once you get far enough away from it; strength and character building; consciousness raising; karma; education you didn't have to pay for; life experienced.

WHAT ARE YOUR PAST FAILURES, MISTAKES, HURTS, TANKS? GET THEM OUT OF YOUR SYSTEM.

1. **Think about your three favorite screwups.** By "favorite," I mean the biggest doozers. They were such fiascos that you just gotta love 'em. Can't come around to reliving your F-ups quite yet? Then just pick the first screwups that come to mind.

2. **What did you learn?** Cynicism won't get you very far here. Truthfully and philosophically ask yourself what you learned. What were your eyes opened to that they weren't before? How were you made stronger by the experience?

3. **Can you see a pattern in the lessons you learned?** Annoyingly, this is also referred to as "repeating lessons." Humans can't seem to avoid making the same mistakes more than once. Bless us.

continues on next page

4. How did what you learned change the way you approach things?

It's only a lesson if it shifted your perspective or the way that you behave.

Things you could do when you're done the purge:

Write HA-HA-HA-HA-HA-HA-HA! in big letters across your page. Tear it up into teeny-tiny pieces. *Burn it!* Start a fire with it! Mail it to yourself with a love letter extolling all of your many virtues.

GLORY BOARDING

WORKSHEET

What are your victories + accomplishments? Sing your praises. If you're feeling too shy to blow your own horn, answer like your BFF or the person who loves you most would answer. Go back as far in your life as you need to for evidence of greatness. This is your résumé of wonder. You:

Inspired:

Launched:

Earned:

Graduated:

Wrote:

Produced:

Raised:

Wrangled:

Traveled:

Motivated:

Sold:

Bought:

Gave:

Made:

Won:

Organized:

Transformed:

Discovered:

Keep going. What else have you done, been, or created?

When you're done creating your glory board: Post it where you can see it. Read it before bed and then pay close attention to your dreams. Rewrite your bio. *Burn it!* Set it free! There's more where that came from.

imagine conjuring

reverie dreams

aspiring visions

hopes wishes

manifesting

fantasies conceived

SESSION 6

vision-
eering

We can still astonish the gods in humanity
And be the stuff of future legends,
If we but dare to be real,
And have the courage to see
That this is the time to dream
The best dream of them all.

—Ben Okri, *Mental Flight*

Our dreams and desires define us, whether they are broken, scarcely remembered, on the verge of reality, or in full bloom. Dreams pilot our choices and shape the landscape of our lives.

We get so many societal messages about what the Right Dream is that it gets hard to decipher what our *own* dream is.

The pandemic that we have of overconsumption is directly related to this concept of dreaming big, bigger, biggest-possible *big*. Big can be bountiful, but what if your dream is to live simply—to have enough? Not *more* than enough—but enough.

The trouble with dreams hinged to goals is that many goal-setting lists are as one-dimensional as shopping lists: get house by the water with hardwood floors; get married; have two kids, preferably twins; run a half marathon. Attaining these things could be the work of your soul or a mindless pursuit.

Are your aspirations a vocational impulse or a competitive sport? Are you trying to impress your dead ancestors or leave your mark on the world?

If your goals aren't synced with the substance of your heart, then achieving them won't matter much.

DREAMING FOR REAL

COP TO DREAM FATIGUE

Sometimes you just get worn out from imagining and aiming—especially if you're a hopelessly romantic go-get-'em type of entrepreneur . . . years of hard work, failures that lead to success, success that leads to failures, loves lost, midcourse corrections.

I've had times in my career where after I left a venture, I could hardly bear to think about profit margins and new connections. I just wanted to write sutras and make soup. Burnout is the ideal time to take a dream hiatus and take stock. Move slowly in the shifting terrain of ambition and idealism. It will be tempting to make plans for what's next, but resist and be still. Go into Savasana. At the end of most yoga classes there is time for Savasana, or the corpse pose. You just lie flat on your back, breathe, and *integrate*. The purpose is that all the work you just did is metabolizing. It's taking effect. We need more Savasana in our lives to integrate what we're learning.

When you fess up to being tired of ever-aiming, the dream fatigue will start to lift and new notions will find their way to you.

HOST A DREAM FUNERAL

It's good to declutter your aspirations every once in a while. Enter the Annual Dream Funeral.

The year that Alexandra was a particularly dark and broody teen (think: *Black Swan*–esque with a green Mohawk), her family's trials also included the death of an uncle, lung surgery for a sibling, and generally a lot of troublesome juju. Her mother decided that it was time to do some formal letting go. "New Year's Eve, Mama Bear brought out a sage stick and told me, my dad, my little sis, and my big bro that we were going to write down things/beliefs/feelings/patterns/perceptions/goals/dank and dusty dreams that we needed to *release* on little pieces of paper, light them on fire, and scatter the ashes," she explains.

I know Alexandra's people. They are a sophisticated folk of high intelligence and talent, so this was a radically woo-woo tactic. "We grumbled a bit (we were slightly unwilling hippies in training), but we did it . . . and it was potent.

"It became an annual Dream Funeral tradition, and over the years, we augmented the ceremony with beer and watching *The Big Lebowski*." Kinda makes you want to be adopted by them, doesn't it?

The Annual Dream Funeral has expanded to include a second step. After scorching your old dreams, write down a new dream, or rather, a single word that represents the new world order. Last year, Alexandra chose the word *voltaic*. She's like that.

THE PSYCHEDELICS OF DREAMING

How you get so fly? . . .
from not being afraid to fall out the sky.

—Jay-Z, "Beach Chair"

You've got to cross the old boundary lines to retrieve new information. If you want a vital outcome, you need vitalized input. You gotta dance, shake it up, go extreme, get off your chain, and then come back to center, where both possibility and practicality synergize.

Promise me that you'll suspend all pragmatism for the purpose of this next exercise. This is not the time to be reasonable, agreeable, or conventional. Where we're going, cynicism is an illegal substance.

If you've done your share of psychedelics or ever watched three Fellini films consecutively, this won't be too much of a stretch. If not, you'll have to call forth the funk factor in your DNA. It's time to trip. You should probably turn the lights off and lie on the floor. Go ahead, I'll wait for you.

What if you dropped some acid and did your goal setting? Or wrote out your bucket list right after you went skydiving and were still high on adrenaline? Just imagine being off in **a thrilled, altered state** as you start mapping out your future.

You'd get out of your box and stomp on it. Colors might explode from where you used to see obstacles. You could be feeling invincible— sporting superhero gear and a Lady Gaga attitude. You'd be artistically mad and damn sexy, making Olympian evocations of the universe. You would be seeing a life that's lit up and you'd be loving it.

Go to the edge, beyond reason. What would be so amazing that you feel shy to even consider it? Where's the rush of absurdity? How much happiness could you stand? What would surprise even you? Feel the high of the extreme dream. You should be peaking right about now.

DREAM TEAM

If you "follow your bliss . . . you will begin to meet people who are in the field of your bliss, and they open the doors to you," said Joseph Campbell, explaining his theory of the "invisible hands" that help you through life.

While you're still tripping on the Milky Way of potential, call in your invisible elders, angels, or faith leaders. Imagine hanging out with the wisdom keepers or titans of your industry—your idols. Now assume that you are their contemporary—that you've earned your place alongside them.

Ask for their grittiest stories and advice, just as you would a new best friend. Jam with them. Observe. Tell them your ideas, give them your pitch, sing them your song. Pay close attention to how they respond. What do they tell you?

GET CRAZY REAL

Now, wind it down, back to Earth. How did it feel to be grandiose? Stimulating or angsty? Did anyone enter your dream and try to highjack it with negativity? What in your trip of dreams felt like you could taste it, reach it? What felt like it was already in progress? What made you feel calm and readied?

You may have found some courage or sagacity on the other side of the extreme dream. You may have imagined new possibilities. You may be thinking *waaay* bigger—or smaller, as in more precise. Either way, you'll be closer to knowing what superpowers of your own that you want to focus on developing.

After you've tripped the light fantastic, you need to put on your sensible walking shoes and just start from where you are. The rest of these sessions is about doing just that: putting fear in its place, saying no to energy drains, calling in the best forces, and combining love with intelligence to make things happen.

VISUALIZE REALITY

I want to try an exercise in refined visualization with you. This is going to require that you think like a wizard. Work with me. Don a persona if that helps: Merlin, Hermione, Harry, Morgan le Fay. Think: alchemical superpowers.

First and most obviously, wizards believe in magic. You have to believe it to see it. Secondly, they trust in the knowledge of all the wizards who have gone before them. They know they're not alone in their pursuits—it's been proven that this magic stuff really works.

Thirdly, and most important for our visualization purposes, wizards operate on the assumption that if they deliver their spell correctly, they'll get the results they want. They wield their wands with certainty. Cast spell, get desired result. Simple.

Wizards assume success. Master manifesters don't "wish" or "hope" that their magic is going to be effective. They know it will be. They rely on the science of it. They believe that on some dimension, another reality already exists and all they need to do is bring that manifestation down to Earth. Pluck.

Wizards aren't in the business of visualizing "what's possible." They're in the business of visualizing results.

This is where some well-intended guided visualizations go astrally astray. It happens a lot at the end of a yoga class, or a special planetary event when someone gets the microphone. "Close your eyes." (*Uh-huh.*) "Deep breath." (*Uh-huh.*) "See your dream before you." (*I can see it. Crystal clear.*) "Now . . . [insert New Age chimes and slightly evangelical tone] . . . know that your dream is *possible*! . . . And open your eyes." And that's it—a visualization with no destination.

"Possible" is foreplay. And fantasizing about foreplay is not half as effectual as fantasizing about going all the way.

Ready your wands.

What do you want? Think of one thing. Got it in your mind?

Abracadabra. It's done. Whoomp, there it is! Somewhere in the universe, it already exists. See how clear it is? You don't have to descend any crystal elevators to get closer to it. You don't need to burn any karma to have it appear in front of you. You don't even need to feel worthy, necessarily—none of that wading and waiting. Just exercise this belief (and yes, it's magical thinking): Somewhere in the cosmos, in the grand bazaar of life, in your very own postal code, what you want is already in existence, waiting for you to pick it up or, better yet, to call and have it delivered.

Keep your wand up. There's always more magic to work.

While you're in the zone of make-believe let's extract some intel. **That image of success that you're seeing may have something to show you**—some how-tos or coordinates, perhaps. This is the coolest part of visualizing things as done deals: You can ask the vision for some clues to making it real. "So, hunky lover babe who laughs at my jokes, wants to have kids, and has been to therapy, tell me, where might I find you?" Answers could range from *Three years from now* to *Look within* to *Seventh and Main*. I believe that all visions come with a how-to strategy if you look more closely at them. Sometimes those strategies are revealed in detailed napkin drawings; other times the vision will whisper *Wait and see.*

And another cool thing about visualizing "Done!" is that **when you get a closer look at your dreams, you may decide to back away from them.** I once thought I wanted a particular business deal to happen. I imagined the website, the response, the results. It was very clear in my mind. I knew in my cells that I could just pick that dream off the shelf and run with it. But when I sat with it for a while and felt how it would affect my life, I decided to move on to the next reality that was ripe for the picking . . . something more my size.

You're never obligated to a dream or a belief. The business of affirmations and visualization is a mind game. Ante up.

SHARE YOUR DREAM

Because dreams tend to be so precious and potent, many people keep their dreams to themselves. A dream is a sacred thing to share, and doing so melts boundaries and calls forth commonalities and resources of all kinds.

VISUALIZED SENSATIONS

Visualizing Possibility = striving, maybe, reach, stretch, could, trying, hit or miss, up for interpretation, deliberation, incomplete, out there, the resounding feeling that there's still so much to do.

Visualizing Done = achievement that you can walk into, the sensation of satisfaction and fulfillment, a reason to celebrate, serious calm, expectation you can wrap your head around, a vision that calls you to stand up straight.

When you know someone's dream you look at that person differently—with more tenderness, respect, familiarity, sympathy, and generosity than before. Look at everyone you meet this week and actively think to yourself, "I wonder what their dreams are?" Ask at least one person what his dream is. You can do it subtly, like, "Where do you see yourself in five years?" or "What did you want to be when you were growing up?" Or you can just go direct: "So, like, what's your big dream?" So many people never get asked that. Even fewer are really listened to when they answer.

The guy in the cubicle next to you may be working on a novel about extraterrestrials and espionage. Your sister might be fantasizing about her own cabaret breakout performance. Your postal carrier may be patenting the next great invention. Make no assumptions about your partner, your workmate, or the bus driver—everyone has a dream in them.

Small, mighty, seemingly impossible, or simply pure . . . when you know what someone's dream is, your perspective leans toward openness.

I dream of Morocco and Paris, and a koi pond in the backyard. Making art, supporting art, learning art. Late-night talks with soul sisters who make me feel crazy blessed and motivated. Stage presence. Books and more books. Film. Belly laughs. I dream about communion. My man. Our son. Always. I dream of sitting around a fire with leaders and lovers of progress. Being able to give yeses that open doors and new dimensions for people. I dream of tenderness and innovation.

I dream of invitations that humble me, and magical connections with people I recognize on a cellular level. I dream that we band together to leverage change. I dream of feeling more electric and sweet every single day.

Mostly, I dream of being amazed.

How 'bout you?

VISION PROMPTING

W O R K S H E E T

What are your dreams?

For each dream, finish this thought:

I want this because . . .

Repeat the thought until you feel like you've hit on the heart of the matter.

Which dreams make you flush with excitement
or be still with peace?

What if none of these dreams is close to your heart?

Are you going to let any of these dreams go?

Who will you share your dream with?

Who already knows about your dream?

Which dreams will you choose to realize?

DREAM ANALYSIS

W O R K S H E E T

Pick one dream and explore . . .

Three reasons why your dream is unreasonable or the odds are
stacked against you.

Three ultraoptimistic and positively affirmative thoughts that
instantly dissolve the bad vibes associated with the so-called
unreasonable nature of your dream.

Three persuasive, potentially outrageous actions that will
create forward traction.

challenging arduous

stuck testing

gripped doubt

difficulties growth

overcome

SESSION 7

fear
+ other
tough
stuff

There will always be suffering.
But we must not suffer over the suffering.

—Alan Watts, Zen master

RESPECT YOUR FEAR

Here's an understatement for you: Being true to yourself is not always easy. Maybe that's why they call it the road less traveled. Maybe that's why Sinatra belted out "My Way" with such badass pride.

For fear of not being accepted, we tailor our personality, mince our words, and carve our opinions to fit in. It takes courage to be creative, vocal, vulnerable—and it takes stamina, because if you want the best out of life, life will demand the best out of you—over and over again.

When you go for genuine, there will be tough choices and eleventh-hour changes. There will be misunderstandings, uncomfortable silences, and, frequently, isolation. There are plenty of things to fear.

Fear is inevitable, natural, and immensely useful. On a physical level, the fear instinct serves to keep us alive. See bear. Fear bear. Get in the SUV and drive away from bear. On a psycho-spiritual level the sensation of fear can actually serve to keep us self-aware. It's a very powerful indicator of where we are contracting, projecting, reaching, risking, sensing darkness.

Trying not to be scared is like trying not to be curious. You can't banish it from your psyche, so you may as well learn to rule it.

We want to notice fear and meet it directly while it's still an emotion, not a behavior. We want to confront or comfort, diffuse and transform it before it seeps into our actions and starts running the show. But what often happens is that we criticize ourselves for being fearful in the first place. *I should be stronger. I'm weak. I should be more confident by now. If this were the right thing to do, I wouldn't be so scared.* It's a vicious cycle of denying what is. You're scared. Start there. Look it in the eye. If you deny it, it's going to keep grabbing at your pant leg, gnawing on your peace of mind, begging to be paid attention to—managing you.

FEAR IS ONE OF MANY EMOTIONS—ALL OF WHICH YOU CAN PRIORITIZE

Imagine that you're a team coach and you're giving your emotions a pep talk before the game. "So how's everyone feeling about the game?" you shout.

Enthusiasm shouts back, "I am stoked! Can't wait to get on the field!" and pumps the air with his fists, smiling, looking to everyone to smile. Anxiety is pacing at the back of the room, in his own world, and looks up briefly to say, "I'm so scared I could puke," and keeps on pacing. Abandonment Issues says, "Look, if we don't score in the first quarter, we should take the ball and go home—end it before they do, you know. But, hey, I'm in!" As the coach, you're nodding, listening to each player intently, and assessing which players to put in the lead for your best chances of victory.

Fear stands up. "Are y'all crazy? If I lose this game, I'll never play in this town again." And then Fear starts picking on the other players. "Enthusiasm, it just ain't natural to be that happy; you gotta get real. And Anxiety! Shit, if you get on the field and have a freeze attack, we all go down."

Finally you step in, "All right, McFearstein, we appreciate your point of view, and you've got some good points. Now let's listen to the others." Just like all of your emotions, Fear just wants to be seen and heard.

Confidence (who is also the team captain) says, "I'm feeling steady. If we stay focused, this win is ours. And when we win, the offers will start pouring in." Insecurity says, "If you want me on the bench, I, I understand, Coach." *Well, if that's where you want to be, then that's where you'll be,* you think to yourself.

Pragmatic shrugs and nods at the same time: "Odds are stacked in our favor. Anything could happen." Love raises her hand. "Listen, you're all fucking amazing! And I believe in every single one of you!" Woot.

Time to drop some truth bombs, Coach. Time to lead, not accommodate. You can't let Fear steal more airtime. And Anxiety is hanging out on the edge distracting everyone. Here's how it's got to go down: "I echo what Love said. You're all amazing. We're contenders. Enthusiasm, you're in front; Confidence and Pragmatic have got your back. Abandonment Issues, your job is to trust your instincts. You *will* know when it's right to pass the ball—we trust you. Anxiety, you're alert, and we need that on the team. You need to stay close to Confidence. The important thing for you to do is just stay in the game—keep playing.

"Fear, thanks for looking out for us. Yep, we could fail, it's possible. This is risky. But we'll come out on top no matter what, because that's who we are. You've done your job, and now you'll be playing from the bench."

When you can see fear as just an emotion that's hanging out with all of your other emotions, you gain some clearer perspective. It's not superior, and it's not even inferior. It's just an emotion that you can choose to focus on or not.

But fear is a persistent bugger. Pay attention to it, but whatever you do . . .

DO NOT DO WHAT FEAR TELLS YOU TO DO

Buddhist nun Pema Chödrön tells a parable about a young warrior woman who was told by her teacher that she had to do direct battle with Fear. Understandably, she was terrified of Fear's wrath. Before the battle, she respectfully asked Fear if she could go into battle with him. This is key. If we approach Fear itself with antagonism (*What the hell do you want?*) or fake bravado (*I'm not frightened of you*), then we're weakening ourselves before we even get into the ring. Fear has teeth, and like any opponent with the potential to kick your ass, Fear deserves your respect. Hostility is an energy sucker. Concentrate. Stay in your integrity; it's your main source of strength.

Then the warrior had the good sense to actually ask Fear, "How can I defeat you?" Brilliant strategy. From qualifying for a mortgage and getting the job, to keeping the love of your life from walking away, just look Fear in the eye and ask, *What's it going to take?* The very act of being courageously sincere and direct is going to release helpful endorphins for you. You are now officially in it to win it.

Fear replied: "My weapons are that I talk fast, and I get very close to your face. Then you get completely unnerved, and you do whatever I say. If you don't do what I tell you, I have no power. You can listen to me, and you can have respect for me. You can even be convinced by me. But if you don't do what I say, I have no power."

You can listen to Fear . . . You can measure the advice of your friends. You can feel your palms sweat and your stomach turn.

But if you don't do what Fear says . . . you'll go ahead and speak up, you'll sign up, you'll buy, you'll sell, you'll jump.

You can have respect for Fear . . . You can know the facts, study the policies, and review history.

But if you don't do what Fear says . . . You can ask for exceptions. You can choose to ignore the statics. You can forge ahead.

You can even be convinced by Fear . . . You can believe that no matter how much you change, your relationship might be doomed.

But if you don't do what Fear says . . . You can return to love—with more daring, greater vulnerability, and deeper truth.

Fear will tell you to contract. Open.
Fear will tell you to plow ahead. Pull back and wait.
Fear will tell you to not rock the boat. Dive in.

THE FEAR OF BEING CRITICIZED

Criticism is something we can avoid easily
by saying nothing, doing nothing,
and being nothing.

—Aristotle

It's said that what people fear the most is death, and after that, it's public speaking. In the nooks and crannies of many of our fears (save for fear of heights and spiders) is the ubiquitous fear of being criticized. It's why we keep our mouth shut, why we lose sleep, and why some people die with their song still inside of them.

If you're putting yourself out there in any way, with almost any degree of courage or chutzpah, criticism is part of the deal. Not an easy part. Sometimes crushing, sometimes spurring, but inevitable.

P.S. YOU'RE NOT GOING TO DIE

Here's the white-hot truth: If you go bankrupt, you'll still be okay. If you lose the gig, the lover, the house, you'll still be okay. If you sing off-key, get beat by the competition, have your heart shattered, get fired . . . it's not going to kill you. Ask anyone who's been through it.

At one time or another you're going to act like a shabby loser idiot and some criticism will be in order. Arrogance, recklessness, wastefulness, lack of care. Pick any of your finer moments in history that still make you wince. You probably had some push back coming to you.

Sometimes we don't necessarily "earn" criticism by falling short of expectations. But by the nature of the arena that we play in, we are likely to bump up against it. Leadership, politics, the arts and entertainment, activism—anywhere you're going public with your opinions or where your exposure increases, you're unavoidably opening yourself to critics.

And then there are the times when you're unjustly dissed. You just don't deserve the criticism. Those times can be especially confusing and infuriating.

No matter the reason or the source, criticism is an opportunity for you to practice the fine art of dignity. It can be the ultimate test of your character. It can be a call to be your classiest self. Either way, it's good to have a comeback. Here are a few pointers that you can use for a whole host of unpleasant occasions:

Breathe. Upon being criticized, your lizard brain wants you to clench your fists and start growling. Not only would that be very unattractive, but you also can't think clearly when your energy is all clamped up and snarly. It's counter to primal instincts, but you need to take a deep, softening breath so that the pain has room to move through and out of you, and so you get some oxygen to your head. **You sustain less injury when you do *not* brace for impact. That's why they call it "rolling with the punches."**

Admit that criticism stings. "Eeeshk. That's hard to hear. But I'm up for it." Honesty when criticized is a great equalizer and a show of maturity—even if you have to fake it and then go bawl your eyes out in your car.

Don't react immediately. Sometimes it's best to just listen and

It's often best to do the *opposite* of what your fear is telling you to do ■

reservedly say, "I've heard you. Let me process what you've said and I'll get back to you tomorrow." Many of us are so adrift from our deep sensitivity that it takes some time to clearly know how we feel. So just take the time. It's better than giving a half-cocked reaction that you'll regret. But if you do say something you regret, or you don't say what you think you should have . . .

Go back to it. Feel free to bring it up again, even if it was a closed subject. *I thought more about what you said and I just wanted to let you know that . . . you really are an asshole.* Juuust kidding. The point is that it's better to clear the air after the fact, than it is to bury your feelings.

Be compassionate with your criticizer. This calls for some Buddha-level enlightenment and some old-fashioned objectivity. Try to appreciate the position that the other person is in. Giving honest criticism is no fun for most people, and it's often a case of "This is going to hurt me as much as it might hurt you." There's a decent chance that your critic fretted over how best to deliver the feedback to you.

Consider the source. As Ralph Waldo Emerson put it, to succeed is "to earn the appreciation of honest critics." So, first, you need to consider your source and their motivation. If you feel you're being inaccurately criticized, then you need to say so in no uncertain terms. This is tricky because you may be perceived as being defensive. In this case, it's good to collect your thoughts and give a rebuttal that honors your strengths—*I've given freely . . . I've lifted spirits . . . I've brought in new business*—and describes the challenges of the situation. *You've needed a lot of support . . . Morale has been low this season . . . I've been operating on a shoestring budget. . . .*

Accept that criticism creates conflict. Whether it's surmounted in minutes, sincerely welcomed, or takes months to overcome, criticism is confrontational and it often creates friction. Oprah's favorite coach, Martha Beck, dispels any illusions about sugarcoating it: "The nature of conflict means you can't set a boundary and take care of someone else's feelings at the same time." Standing up for yourself means you're not carrying the other person at that moment. You will naturally push against criticism—that is part of examining and assessing it, valuing or rejecting it. Pushing back may get very uncomfortable. Don't expect it to be otherwise. And . . .

Don't take any shit. Sometimes you have to play hardball. I once got a super-crappy performance review from a manager at a retail job. I got on the phone right away and called the big cheese. "There's no way I'm signing this review, and there's no way I'm quitting. I think she's losing her marbles." My heart was racing when I dialed the phone, but I knew I had to do it. As it turned out, I wasn't the only person complaining about the Manager Gone Mad. She left shortly thereafter. And guess who got promoted?

Know your rights. Sometimes there are legalities to consider. Your job may be on the line. If you lip off, and it leads to a dismissal, you'll want to know what your legal and moral rights are. Employers may need to formally warn you in writing, and so forth. You also have the right to be treated with respect no matter how severely you screw up. Criticism given without care is just irresponsible and nasty. Criticism delivered with sensitivity and kindness goes a long way.

Bring closure to it. If you're being asked to improve in some way, then ask for specific, measurable examples. You can't run a race if you don't know where the finish line is.

Say thank you. Whether you've been rightly or wrongly critiqued, say thanks. Thanks for letting me know, thanks for bringing it up, thanks for communicating. Whether you agree or not, it's a learning opportunity and you can muster some gratitude for that.

Be gentle with yourself. Put an ice pack on your ego and order in some comfort food. Give yourself a few minutes or the duration of a cappuccino to mope. Tomorrow is another day, and you'll be ready for it.

DECONSTRUCTING FEAR

WORKSHEET

If you bring forth what is within you, what you bring forth will save you. If you do not bring forth what is within you, what you do not bring forth will destroy you.

—Saint Thomas

Getting clear on what you're scared of can instantly defuse ticking anxiety bombs. This is where you get it out of your system: bankruptcy, unfulfilled potential, trashing your reputation, ending up a spinster, losing it all, a supposedly fatal diagnosis. And then (because we just can't stop there), you're going to apply some simple analysis to it. You may have nothing to fear after all.

This is an incredibly simple and powerful exercise that I learned from the Diamond Approach, a self-realization philosophy developed by A.H. Almaas (a great introduction to his massive body of work is his book *The Unfolding Now*). I respectfully refer to this as the Because Why Inquiry.

Think of something you're afraid of. Got it in your head? Now ask yourself "Why am I afraid of . . . ?" Answer it. Ask again. *Because why?* Answer again—you can give the same answer or a different one, but eventually you'll need to get unstuck and discover another reply for yourself. Keep repeating the *Because why?* question and keep answering it. It's amazing what the basic repetition can dig up as you drill down closer to the source of your fear.

What are you afraid of? "I'm afraid of getting fired."

Why are you afraid of getting fired? "Because the money is good."

Why are you afraid of getting fired? "Because competition in my industry is tough."

Why are you afraid of getting fired? "Because I'd be humiliated."

Why are you afraid of getting fired? "Because I'd have to tell my father."

Why are you afraid of getting fired? "Because my dad would have one more reason to think I'm never going to amount to anything."

Why are you afraid of getting fired? "Because I'll never get the love I want from my father."

Eureka.

This is a powerful exercise to do with another person that you trust. As they keep repeating the *Because why?* question to you, you may have to resist the urge to scream at them, "Stop asking me that!" Avoid brutality. That's not part of the exercise. Ride through the annoyance and your own emotions and you'll crack through some layers to the light of insight.

How do you feel when you see the reasons behind your fears?

learned healing

insight

empowered perspective

integrating wisdom

SESSION 8

comfort-ing failure

Losses aren't cataclysmic if they teach the heart and
soul their natural cycle of breaking and healing. A
real tragedy? That's the loss of the heart and soul
themselves. If you've abandoned yourself in the effort
to keep anyone or anything else, unlearn that pattern.
Live your truth, losses be damned. Just like that,
your heart and soul will return home.

—Martha Beck

THE MISTAKEN MYTH

You've probably surmised by now that I believe that everything happens for a reason. There's order in chaos and all that. But here's my favorite misuse of such holistic positivity: "There's no such thing as a mistake." Ah, yes, spiritualized justifications of poor behavior and human weakness. Like when someone's just lost half of your savings or sneaks out of rehab again and we chalk it up to just another meant-to-be learning opportunity sanctioned by the universe. Of course, the cosmos always has a bigger plan, and blessings can come wrapped in curses. But if we don't face up to our missteps on a very basic level, then we miss the full gift of our humanity and our capacity to make lasting change.

Mistakes happen. Big, dumb, stupid, lazy mistakes. Fat frickin' messes that you will regret for a very long time. And no affirmation or predeterministic thinking will change the fact that you've done gone and fucked up. And when you can get that real about it, you don't need to waste energy protecting your ego or pouring on the sweetener. You can use that energy to clean up the mess and love yourself while you're doing it.

MY VERY FAVORITE

DOOZERS + LOSERS

Devilish angel investors, pissed-off magazine editors, princess-style spending, red flags firmly ignored. I've made some fabulous mistakes in the name of fame, fortune, and reputation management. It is my most earnest wish to save you from a few of them.

ALL HAIL THE EIGHT-SECOND RULE

My personal theory is that you get ample intuitive information about someone in the first, say, eight seconds of meeting them. If your antennae are honed, if you've made a practice of following your instincts, then you know in the first handshake; you know when someone shows up two minutes early or two minutes late; you know from the sound of their voice on the other end of the phone; you know from the tone of their email. Somewhere in your being, **you just know.** Like or dislike. Open or closed. Curious or careful. Eight seconds.

Pay close attention. There is a Buddhist saying:

As in the beginning, so in the middle, so in the end ■

The ancient Greeks used to say, "A beginning is the half of the *all*." By *all* they meant the universe. Things often continue how they start. The click, the comfort, the clarity or the lack thereof, is there at the get-go, and whatever that early dynamic is, it's very likely that it will carry forward to greater or lesser degrees.

Consultant Boy stood me up on our first meeting. He called not one but two days later to reschedule.

"Did he apologize or explain?" I asked my assistant.

"Nope."

I thought he was the only game in town. (*No one* is ever the only game in town.) And that I could teach him some respect. (I'm only soul contracted to do that for my son. Everyone else is required to act like an adult.) And so I ignored his rude entry and—gulp—I hired him. Do I need to tell you how the middle and the end of that story went? In one way or another he continued to stand me up, until it came a-tumblin' down.

When I'm tempted to take shortcuts or ignore warning flags, I remind myself that the most fab, wonderful, sustaining experiences and relationships in my life all began incredibly easily. *Spark! Yes! And Go!*

Examine your first encounters and kickoffs. They may be a micro of the macro. You have oodles of critical information in the beginning if you're paying very close attention. This is the time to establish your healthy boundaries and limits and begin as you wish to proceed.

And if you don't buy it from the Buddha or me, then take it from Maya Angelou, who says, "The first time someone shows themselves to you, believe them." You know it, babe.

FUCK YOUR SO-CALLED PRINCIPLES

The way is light and fluid for the man with
no preferences.

—Lao-tzu

Principles can wreak havoc in your life. Take Galileo. It was the 1600s and the Italian physicist had rightly concluded that the sun does *not* circle the Earth, but rather the Earth circles around the sun. This really pissed off the Catholics in charge. Something about Psalms 104:5, "The Lord set the Earth on its foundations; it can never be moved." Things got nasty. Galileo was tried in court and found guilty of heresy.

They gave him two options. He could "abjure, cure and detest" his theory. Just simply say, "Silly me. The Earth *is* the center of the universe, for the Bible tells me so." Or he could be hanged. Eeny, meany, miny . . . no. Galileo recanted, and spent the rest of his life in house arrest, researching, writing, and building what became the foundations of modern science as we know it. Productive guy. We can be glad that he threw his principles to the wolves and got on with his life.

Principles are so easy to get attached to. They're the glamorous side of having a conscience. But sometimes peace of mind has very little to do with looking good.

Some young TV producers and I were tangled in a very-good-for-them-but-bad-for-me contract. "It's not about the money grab they're going for," I ranted to my lawyer. "I don't care about the money. It's about the principle of the matter. What they're doing is so wrong and they bloody well know it."

"So you want to drag this out for months because of your principles?" he said. "You want to sink a few more grand into this because of your *principles*? I've had a lot of clients over the years that have made themselves sick, wrecked their marriages, or drained their finances to protect their so-called principles.

"Of course the producers are wrong. They're greedy twits. You could countersue and probably crush them. But fuck your principles and get on with your life."

And so I did.

Do you want
to be right, or
do you want
to be free? ▪

GUARANTEES ARE NO GUARANTEE

You're an optimist, right? You believe in love at first sight, synchronicity, human potential, and the search for intelligent life. Me, too. But after a few too many early hires, resented workloads, and, um, a speedy marriage proposal that I had no business accepting, I've become a big fan of optimistic but incremental commitment. *Mature,* I know. But it's not as boring and restrictive as it may sound. It's power generating.

Love everyone. Trust few. Paddle your own canoe.

—Anonymous

The incremental commitment formula goes like so: The more it works, the more you give. Simple. You don't invest in hope. You respond to results. You earn your respect and you let the people around you earn theirs.

Cassie thought she was a killer lady boss. "Oh, yeah, I thought I was hot stuff. Wheeling my deals, getting offers in by midnight, hiring, firing. I loved to make big promises and crazy commitments—both about what I could produce for the company and what I wanted people to produce for us." Cassie rolled her eyes and did one of those snortle laughs—proving once again that the *I can SO laugh at myself* snortle coming from a powerful woman is super-sexy and endearing. "So I'd offer people big, sweeping deals right off the bat. Just to wow 'em. I'd give them a fat salary and a great parking spot and start talking about how much cash they'd be raking in in a year or two because we'd be sure to hit our sales targets.

"Of course, sometimes this would pay off. But let's face it, winners are rare and shit happens, so when it was clear in week two that someone just wasn't going to work out, I'd tend to ignore the signs and keep trying to work it out because the promises were so . . . *promised*."

Been there. "I know this one so bad, sister," I jumped in. "Remember when I booked a distant future trip to Maui with that guy I'd met just the weekend before? I was so banking on him being a full-tilt winner. Lost my deposit on that one." Snortle.

Cassie is an introspective mover and shaker, and she had her aha moment eventually. "It was really just a lack of trust on my part . . . and probably self-worth issues if I'm really real about it. I thought if I showed up first with a *lot* to offer, then they'd come through. I overcompensated to try to get what I wanted out of people. It just weakens everyone and mostly me and my budget."

It took some hope and restraint, but Cass started bringing people onto her team with far less offered up front. She pretty much erased the word *guaranteed* from her vocabulary. New players were offered three months to make the grade. Bonuses were based on performance. Cassie curbed her quick-to-give nature, and when people actually delivered the results, she then let her gratitude cheer the loudest. Her pragmatism *and* enthusiasm rode side by side.

One-step-at-a-time commitment creates traction. It's not about withholding. The withholding posture in any kind of relationship is just nasty and manipulative. Leave that for kidnappers and ransomers. Rather, incremental commitment is about being responsive to reality. This approach gives you leeway for mutual accountability, for prerogatives to be exercised, and for the self-motivated players to motivate themselves.

Speaking of grown-up teamwork . . .

DOMAINS OF RESPONSIBILITY
FOSTER TRUST

Consensus building can be a total drag. It's a very likely progenitor for a lot of mediocrity that happens in organizations—and relationships for that matter. Leadership isn't necessarily about getting agreement. Leadership often requires you to direct people who, as devoted and qualified as they may be, are not as fully informed and infused—either with the facts, the wisdom, or instinct—as you should be. Trying to convince everyone that you're right is not the best use of energy.

When you all have to "agree," you'll start to hesitate. You'll weigh your decisions more. And you will miss opportunities. When each person can be fully empowered to take creative action in their corner of the world, you get smarter, more responsible actions. You've got to trust the people on your team to be brilliant and screw up and make things happen—which they'll have more time to do if they're not busy getting buy-in from everyone.

What you need to agree on is what you need to agree on. Beyond that, each person is good and free to blaze new trails.

I've been a part of some fantastic collaborations. We were like a deft sailing team, each knowing when to pull the lines or grab the tiller. We cruised. I've had some wonky unions where we were the blind leading the blind, stumbling on expectations and codependencies, but managing to make progress. And I've been half of a duo that looked picture-perfect but had some flaws beneath the gloss. As much as I long for fluidity in creative partnering, I've become an advocate of domains of responsibility: The buck's gotta stop with someone.

Consensus can create mediocrity. When you and your

partner(s) decide that you have to agree on everything, it can stymie decision making, slow you down, foster risk aversion, and weaken your strategizing. When you *have* to agree, you tend to avoid things that might cause *disagreements*. Not good.

When, however, you agree that one person has the final say in a particular area, here's what happens, ideally: The person with the final call is extra-thoughtful, weighs the options, does their homework—and trust is nurtured. Teamwork isn't about harmony at all times; it's about covering all the bases so you can win the bigger game by letting each person exercise their true individual strengths—and carrying the success and the failure together.

So figure out who's in charge of what—the marketing, the money, the staff, the front end, the back end, the brand. Allow for creative tension, and give everyone enough space to leap, to lose, and to take their charge to a whole new level.

TRANSFORMING THE TOUGH STUFF

When your fear touches someone's pain, it becomes
pity; when your love touches someone's pain, it becomes
compassion. To train in compassion, then, is to know
all beings are the same and suffer in similar ways,
to honor all those who suffer, and to know you are
neither separate from nor superior to anyone.

—Stephen Levine

Negative emotions crystallize in our psyches, they contribute to clogged arteries, and they junk up the morphogenetic field, so it's cosmically diligent to take responsibility for shifting them. Seeing clearly in fear and darkness is one of the victories of awakening. **But what if we took it one step further and made an effort to actually transform our pain into something beautiful?** What if we went full out and made an effort to transform *other people's pain* into something beautiful?

Tonglen is Tibetan for "sending and taking," and it's a Buddhist meditation technique for overcoming fear and suffering. Tonglen is one of the most empowering, life affirming, and truly creative practices I've experienced. It's best summed up as this:

Breathe in for all of us and breathe out for all of us. Breathe in suffering—yours, others, the world's. Breathe out compassion—for yourself, for others, for the world.

The tonglen practice is a method for connecting with suffering—ours and that which is all around us—everywhere we go, and dissolving the tightness of our heart. As Pema Chödrön describes it, "Primarily it is a method for awakening the compassion that is inherent in all of us, no matter how cruel or cold we might seem to be. . . . However, we often cannot do this practice because we come face-to-face with our own fear, our own resistance, anger, or whatever our personal pain, our personal stuckness happens to be at that moment." Tonglen suggests a radical approach to our habitual ways of resisting pain and all things negative: **Absorb it and therefore transform it.** The approach is sometimes referred to as "using what seems like poison as medicine."

Like all Buddhist practices, there are layers of nuances and layers of meaning to this form of meditation. I'm not a studied practitioner of Tibetan Buddhism, and I have no intention of taking vows, but here's what I've found works for me, spiritual mutt that I am.

HOW TO TONGLEN

1. **Get yourself into a calm and centered meditative state of mind.** (I've done tonglen on a meditation cushion and on the crosstown bus; for an hour and for three minutes. There's no need to get formal about it if your intention is clear.)
2. Focus on the suffering of a specific person or on your own personal pain. **Breathe in the pain.** Let it be vivid. Let it be heavy or smothering or whatever it needs to be.

   Some teachers suggest imagining black light streaming into your heart, or calling on the power of enlightened beings to help open your heart to compassion.
3. **Breathe out relief** to that person or yourself—whatever you feel would be the healing counter to the suffering. Send out any feelings that encourage openness and ease.

This is where some teachers suggest envisioning white light extending out of your heart.

Who (or what) do you know that's hurting? A child. A friend in her first round of chemotherapy. Your racist neighbor who doesn't even know he's suffering. Victims of rape and human trafficking. One of many impoverished nations. Starving polar bears. Our oceans and rivers.

Breathe in the wish to take away all their pain and fear. Then, as you breathe out, send them happiness, ease, care, or whatever you feel would relieve their pain.

You can start with your own fear and tough stuff, or that of those around you. Breathe in the worst thing that ever happened to you. That sunk feeling. That thing you wish you could take back. Recapitulate it in breaths: the blackness, the sickness, the fibrous seething rage, the sticky-scratchy, inconsolable weight of it. Take in the unbearableness. You may want to escape. Press on. Go beyond the grip. Inhale the pain in to your every cell. You won't die. You're going to expand. Keep breathing.

You're on the verge of a miracle.

Now breathe out joy. Soothing golden warmth. Luminous flying birds of clarity. Electric rays of smiling karate chops. Feel your lungs as powerful creative engines of healing and righteousness. Pulsate rapture. Let happiness emerge from the fractures. Let scar tissue become bridges that lead to a festival of relief and dancing. See joy. Feel joy. Hear joy. Sing joy. Breathe love into every cell of the situation.

Now do it for other people's suffering. Please. For that homeless man on the street, in winter. Cold and demoralized. Inhale his agony. Exhale comfort and transformation. The jobless folks with families to feed. Cancer patients fighting to live. People gone mad. Soldiers who kill and the families they destroy. Take in the wreckage. Turn it into light and give back compassion and tenderness.

When your heart is heavy, when you want to feel alive . . . breathe.

This practice may shatter you. But wouldn't that be grand? To be shattered? To be so immensely open that you'd feel the truth: that you're really as selfless, as loyal, as creative, as tender, as strong . . . as all of us.

Acknowledge the dark.
Take the light into your own hands.
Transmute.
Fear less.

COMFORT ZONING

W O R K S H E E T

The thing about being afraid or in crisis mode is that we can get so spun out that we forget where the emergency exit or the rip cord is. Where's your bridge over troubled water? Who ya gonna call? How do you spell *relief*? Lunch with your best friend, a visit to church, a call with your mastermind group, a few laps in the pool, silence?

Make a list of your soul vitamins so you can mentally, or literally, refer to it when the going gets rougher than tough.

When I do the following, I am guaranteed to feel close to 100 percent improved, lighter, and focused:

When I do the following, I will likely feel a sense of relief or improvement:

As for downing a carton of cookie dough ice cream, drunk dialing your former flame, sneaking a smoke in the airplane bathroom, watching *Gene Simmons Family Jewels* reruns instead of going to yoga class, and all manners of vengeful vandalism . . . let's put that "comfort list" in its place.

Even though I *think* that doing the following things will bring me relief and comfort, they actually aren't helpful at all:

strengthened clarified

boundaries respected

permission granted

onward

SESSION 9

no,
thank you.
yes,
please.

A lot of the time, it's better to quit than to be the hero.

—Jason Fried +
David Heinemeier Hansson,
authors of *Rework*

NO MAKES WAY FOR YES

One of Frank Gehry's first buildings was a shopping mall, the Santa Monica Place. It was rigidly geometric and pale pink. Think bad eighties jungle gym. To please his investors he went L.A. style with a twist. He hated it.

Meanwhile, for his own creative outlet, Frank went full-out "Gehry" on building his own home: sloping roofs, curvaceous windows, jutting peaks. Wildly organic. The night of the grand opening of the Santa Monica Place, the president of the real estate company that had hired Frank was at Frank's home for a dinner party. As Frank describes it, this short conversation changed the course of his life:

Real estate exec, looking around Gehry's house, awestruck:
"What the hell is this?"

Frank: "Well, I was experimenting, you know, playing with it."

Exec: "You must like it if it's your house. You do like this, right?"

Frank: "Yeah. I'm happy with how it turned out."

The moment you say yes to acting on your desire is the real beginning ■

Exec: "So, then . . . the building that you just did for us—the shopping mall—you can't possibly like that."

Frank: "You're right, I don't."

Exec: "Then why'd you do it?"

Frank: "Because I need to make a living."

Pause.

Exec: "Well, stop it. Don't do that kind of work anymore."

Frank: "Yeah, you're right."

They shook hands that night and decided to quit every project they were working on, which was a rather big deal, since they were employing forty people at the time.

"It was like jumping off a cliff. It was an amazing feeling," Frank says. "I was so happy from then on."

Even after his big-yes moment, there were failures for Frank. He was supposedly cash-strapped more than once. He bid on projects that he never got. He had to can staff. He seriously questioned his own judgment. But he never did another building that he didn't absolutely love creating.

The moment you say yes to acting on your desire is the real beginning. It's not when you give your notice or when your novel is off the press. Do you want a career that amazes even you? Then say yes. Do you want a love life brimming with adoration and the sweet stuff? Then say yes. If you start to tell me why it's not possible, or how bad you want it but you don't know how to get it—then you don't want it bad enough. *Maybe* isn't going to cut it. *Maybe* clogs up the dream machine.

But before you can say yes to the good stuff . . . you probably need to learn to say no to all that other stuff.

THE EUPHORIA OF ADMITTING WHEN IT SUCKS

REFRAMING *QUIT*

It's not so much quitting as . . . stopping, ceasing, retiring, putting it to rest, letting it fly, moving on, phasing out, bringing to a conclusion, taking a bow, changing course, clarifying, focusing, perfecting, shifting, trading up.

If I just hang in here a little longer, maybe she'll come up to speed. He'll change; I just need to be more flexible. If I really apply myself, I'll learn to love this kind of work. Our sense of duty can blind us to the clues of doom. Just 'fess up—it ain't workin'.

Step 1: Acknowledge what's broke, hurting, brutal, FUBAR'd, perpetually disappointing.

Step 2: **Do not worry about how you are going to fix what's broke.**

Step 3: Reaffirm what's not working so you're really clear on the extent of the suckage. We don't want you talking yourself into happy thoughts just yet. **Just notice what sucks with ruthless honesty. Then—and only then—will solutions emerge.**

It's a momentary rush when you get to the realness. Relief! It's I-know-it-sucks-euphoria. And when you're high on the truth, you get a new vantage point of where to go next.

165

THE SIGNS OF SUCKAGE

RESENTMENT RED ALERT

Success is gritty business, and you've got to hustle your bustle. You've got to eat intensity Wheaties for breakfast. But there's a difference between satisfying rigor and inane slogging. Slogging doesn't work for you in the long run. You collapse.

Forcing yourself to do things that build resentment just makes you full of . . . resentment. What's the good of being disciplined and enduring if you're perpetually perturbed? Vexed, miffed, annoyed, *bitter*. **Resentment is toxic.** It coats your esteem, weighs on your good intentions, and sucks enthusiasm out of every kind of relationship. Over the long haul, resentment yields a good-for-nothing crop of sour grapes. You simply cannot plant seeds of misery today and expect to get a juicy harvest next season.

What do you resent doing, or enduring, and how can you weed it out of your garden—*stat*?

"This one client drove me out of my mind. They didn't understand the concept of 'final decisions,' they waffled, they asked the same questions over and over again. And they were total sweethearts. Great people—they were just afflicted with chronic indecision," explains Chris. "I hung in there for months because they're such good folk. I'd burned so much time handholding that I was basically losing money, but I felt incredibly obligated to complete the project. I finish everything, and I mean *everything*." I can vouch for him. Chris is one of those Highly Responsible, Refreshingly Reliable Humans—a total gift to have in your life. But even superhumans have their limits.

"It got to the point where just one more repetitively perplexed email from them and I wanted to snap my laptop lid off and beat myself with it. While my fingers would be typing, 'Hope this is clear. Sincerely, Chris', my mouth would be yelling, 'What the hell have I been telling you for four months, you illiterate morons!' I was getting deranged with resentment. I turned into, like, a werewolf when I got so much as a text from them. I was losing sleep. I was barking at my kids. I wasn't good to anybody."

The silver bullet? Call it for what it is: crazy making. "I let them know that I gave it my all, and that the decision racked me, but that I just couldn't be of service to them anymore. I returned a month's worth of pay, gave them all of their files, and offered to bring their next contractor up to speed. I took a deep breath when I pressed send, and then I did the karate chop of victory."

Once Chris paid his fee at the Crazy Town tollbooth, something wonderful happened, as it typically tends to when we choose sanity: A dream client showed up the following week with deep pockets and a penchant for decisiveness.

If you can't immediately drop the loathsome and resented tasks from your life, then make a plan to phase them out. You're going to feel like you're flying with your load lightened. Plan for velocity.

SUNDAY-NIGHT ANXIETY

It starts to creep in at about eight o'clock the night before the workweek starts. I believe the Latin term is *Yuckis Lundi Dreadus*. You start thinking about everything waiting for you on Monday. Looming. Targets to hit, important conversations to have, what to wear. How you gonna fake motivated *this* week? Your stomach starts to knot with anticipation, and any chance of savoring your last hours of freedom is strangled.

This is not to be mistaken for performance jitters and healthy, anxious excitement. No, no. This is sheer and indisputable dread.

And it entirely sucks. If you've got a regular case of the *Yuckis*, you need to rethink what happiness means to you. A life where you look forward to each and every day, perhaps?

BLEAK ABSENCE OF SYNCHRONICITY

The entire universe is a great theater of mirrors.

—Alice Bailey

What's life reflecting back to you? When things aren't grooving, when it's one damn thing after the other, then you might start praying for magic signs from the universe. *Dear God, if I'm meant to call him, give me a sign. Two knocks for yes, one for no.*

When you're moving on the soul highway, you don't need to pray for signs; they're everywhere. Synchronicities show up to affirm that you're going in the right direction.

NO EXPLANATION NECESSARY

Me, you, or someone you know:

"I don't want to do it anymore. I'm going to . . . "

Take your pick: *quit, sell, throw in the towel, bag it, sink it, tank it, walk*. You're sure of it. Decision made.

Not so fast. Because once we have quittin' clarity, we tend to get rationalization creep.

Enter that practical voice inside your head, well-intentioned friends, yo' mama: "Now, why would you do that?! . . . [*Take your pick.*] It's good money. It's a great opportunity. You've worked so hard. What will you do without it? Can't you work things out? I mean, *really.*"

And then it happens. You bite the hook. You start to rationalize your decision.

How about this for a rationalization? **It just doesn't feel right.**

That's it. What else is there to explain? How can someone argue with your feelings? They'll try, and maybe they'll help you see things differently and your feelings will effectively shift. But when you know deep down, when you're clear as quartz in sunlight, why sully that lucidity with a complicated justification?

I left a television gig once because it just didn't feel right. I really struggled with all of my options: Quit. Stay. Suck it up. Expand my perspective. A few people thought I was nuts to walk away. It was great exposure, extra money, an easy gig (I filmed it from my home, for God's sake). All true and logical facts.

So then I made the tastiest excuse sandwich about why the job didn't really work for me. *I need to find a babysitter, it interrupts my week flow, it's not what I signed up for, I need a haircut, and I need to focus more on my writing.* All true and logical facts. But in the grand scheme of what I'm capable of, these were all totally lame and absolutely surmountable situations. Pathetic. If something feels right, I'll drive all night in a push-up bra to get there. When something feels right, you put inconveniences in their place. Whatever it takes.

The job felt okay, but I wasn't *really* having fun. It didn't *really* light me up. I didn't *really* look forward to it. When something doesn't feel right, that's reason enough. And that is the only reason that you need to say no to something.

THE CORROSIVE EFFECTS OF
OVERJUSTIFYING YOUR FEELINGS

When you put yourself in a position to justify how you're feeling, you're automatically putting yourself on the defensive. Here's the incredibly important salient point I want to make here: When we go through the process of justifying our feelings and our reasoning for doing something, it's corrosive to our inner integrity and even our logic.

Justifying how you feel about something perpetuates cleverness, and *clever* in my dictionary is not a particularly positive word—it tends to be a bit manipulative; it's slick. Clever people cleverly tell others the clever things they want to hear.

In an effort to prove and protect, you make up reasons that appear to be more important than your so-called refutable instinct. You whine. You nitpick the situation. You start sounding like the wimp you don't want to be instead of the hero that you essentially are. You devise complaints to support your position. You victimize yourself.

When you justify how you feel, you are depressing the stamina and the power of your essential self, creating excuses for your truth. You're abandoning yourself. The more you load rationale on top of your feelings, the more padding you create between you and your most powerful resources. And if you make a habit of keeping your instincts at bay, they tend to stay at bay.

The elegance of "It just doesn't feel right" does not negate the necessity to quit things responsibly and with integrity. Sometimes your character or the situation will demand that you give detailed, precise explanations about why you're leaving a situation, because that's the most compassionate and mature thing to do. Taking the time to explain yourself can be an incredibly compassionate act.

And in that precision you must stay rooted to your heart. Always circle back to explaining how you *feel*. Nobody can argue with how you feel unless you're arguing with yourself.

Hold the excuses. Speak from your heart.

NO REALLY, JUST STOP IT

If you're going to realize your intentions, what you stop doing is just as important as what you start and continue to do. This is where "quitting" crosses over into enlightenment. Stopping = the white space. Stopping = room to run free and create from the deepest place of being without restraint or compromise. Stopping = more time for what matters most. You know how to go, go, go. Stopping, however, is the stuff of smiley Zen masters with all the time in the world.

Stopping what's distracting, draining, or aggravating doesn't require any heavy lifting or extra stamina—just love and self-respect.

SUGGESTED STOP-ITS

1. **Stop checking email obsessively.** Have you heard? If you're checking email every five minutes during the day, you're checking it at least 24,000 times a year.

2. **Stop last-minute, rushing, drag-your-ass trips to the grocery store, bank, and video store.** *Have it delivered.* Get a food delivery service for your organics; the cost isn't much more than gas and parking. Set up direct bank deposits and auto payments. Watch movies online.

3. **Stop doing the tasks that are not in your natural skill set, or suck time from doing what you do best.** *Outsource.* The rise of virtual assistants is a phenomenon that enables you to get anything done for anywhere from $4 to $70 an hour, from India to Nebraska, from Twitter pages to legal docs to having someone order flowers for your grandma's birthday. Get an intern, or put your teens or retired auntie to work. Invest in your freedom.

4. **Stop buying gifts that need to be wrapped and/or mailed.** Buy experiences and gift certificates for things such as concerts and conferences, magazine subscriptions, online music, and books.

5. **Stop being in charge.** Give people a chance to rise to the occasion. Your kid can dress herself. (Rubber boots and surf shorts look great!) Staff can figure out most things. (Mistakes are useful.)

6. **Stop doing it alone.** Team with experts. A great coach, designer, or consultant can create quantum leaps.

7. **Stop subscribing.** Rather than just hitting delete, go through the steps to keep your in-box squeaky clean.

8. **Stop taking home "free" stuff**—pens, kitsch-filled gift bags from networking events, ugly volunteer T-shirts. You will only spend time moving them around or pawning them off at your neighbor's yard sale.

9. **Stop forcing yourself to finish every book you pick up** because you think the ghost of your English teacher is watching. I hereby give you permission to not finish books that suck. (But you're finishing this book, right?)

THE STOP-DOING LIST

W O R K S H E E T

Look back on your year and get very clear about what sucked. What didn't work, got mired in resentment, felt onerous, weighed you deadly down?

All of the above activities serve only to make you busier, or put you *out* of the zone of your true strengths.

What will you stop doing? Effective immediately?

part3

results

design systems art

ideas theories

programs structures

utility crafted

concepts

wisdom informing

SESSION 10

make stuff that feels good to make

I am my best work—a series of road maps, reports, recipes, doodles, and prayers from the front lines.

—Audre Lorde, poet

People who earn the label "creative" are really just people who come up with more combinations of ideas, find interesting ones faster, and are willing to try them out. The problem is that most schools and organizations train us out of those habits.

—Guy Kawasaki, *Reality Check*

SEEING YOUR LIGHT

When it comes to our innate wisdom and expertise, many of us are like fish swimming in water. We're so acclimated to our environment, to the knowledge that buoys us, that we don't even notice it. Consider this: You could be taking your genius for granted.

You know stuff. You know stuff that other people don't know. And when you know stuff that other people do not, you're in a position to be of service. Ideally, you want to be of service to others in a way that feeds your spirit.

I was invited to speak at an association event, and like I do with all of my gigs, I asked the conference planner what she thought the challenge was for the group and what she wanted them to walk away with. "They need to see new opportunities for themselves," she said. Normally, this would be a slam-dunk presentation, since opportunities in niche industries or within a certain type of tribe are easier to spot. But this group was a mash-up of company managers and freelancers, all different ages, outlooks, and specialties.

In one row there was a silver-bearded journalist wearing a purple Shakespeare Festival sweatshirt taking notes on his reporter pad, in pencil. Behind him was a young chicklet who was tweeting from her iPhone: "Does this event, like, have a hashtag?" And in the back row there was my friend Patsy, in her Eileen Fisher black suit, wondering if I'd have anything relevant to say that she could apply to her twenty years in the hospitality industry.

If you can find the commonality in a group, you soften a potentially tough crowd. Whether they knew it or not, they all had the same concerns: How do I use what I've got to advance my career? And how do I stand out?

Here's how: **You leverage what you already know with what turns you on. Your insight + a passion project = hell, yes!**

Here's what I asked my audience of curmudgeons, early adopters, and mavens:

WHAT BUSINESS ARE YOU REALLY IN?

A master in the art of living draws no sharp distinction between his work and his play; his labor and his leisure; his mind and his body; his education and his recreation. He hardly knows which is which. He simply pursues his vision of excellence through whatever he is doing, and leaves others to determine whether he is working or playing. To himself, he always appears to be doing both.

—Lawrence Pearsall Jacks

This is a trick question. Ray Kroc, the founder of McDonald's, asked a class of MBAs what business they thought he was in. "Restaurants.

Food. Hamburgers," they answered, predictably. Nope! Ray countered: "Real estate." The success of McDonald's was predicated on putting actual restaurants in as many locations as possible. The empire wasn't so much about the Big Mac as it was about giving people easy access to the Big Mac. Location, location, location.

You may be an event planner who is really in the business of stress management or trend spotting. Some doctors are more in the business of data dispensing than caretaking. The best hairstylists I know are actually in the healing and empowerment industry, and some of the best receptionists are in the same business as bodyguards—they're protective ninjas. Some project managers exist to motivate. Yoga studios are community builders. Waiters sell charm, residential real-estate agents sell comfort, and we all know that bartenders are really in the therapy business.

Personally, I'm in the wisdom-broadcasting business. I convert information into knowledge, give it my personal perspective, and then deliver it in every format possible. I either give it away for free or I sell it. Make wisdom. Tell people about it.

Not quite sure about your essential line of work? Then ask yourself:

WHAT'S THE EXPERIENCE THAT YOU'RE GIVING TO PEOPLE?

What do you do for them that affects their life or their work, if even for a moment? That might lead you to the heart of your offering.

"Try this on for size," I said to the writers in the audience. "Forget that you're 'writers.' There's a bigger story to your story. Some of you are in the business of adventure, midlife crises, social critique, activism, aspiration. . . . It doesn't matter whether you're writing about a doing Bali on a budget or covering a new celebrity fragrance.

"Assuming that you're speaking from your own voice, you bring a particular slant or paradigm to what you're talking about. And that creates an experience for people—they get empowered to act, they get sobered up by the facts, they get melted by the beauty."

One of the fashion magazine writers took me aside afterward and said, "I write all kinds of articles for a women's fashion magazine. Some of them are really informative self-help stuff, and sometimes I'm just reporting on new designs. But my thing is to make it all lighthearted, you know, a bit whimsical. So I think what I'm really about is being entertaining." We talked awhile longer and I found out that the "entertainment" theme ran through everything she did: how she threw parties, how she approached staff meetings, the touch of costume-glam in how she dressed. She was consistent; she just needed to put a name to it.

WHAT DO YOU LOVE KNOWING ABOUT?

If you have knowledge, let others light their candles in it.

—Margaret Fuller

The answer to this goes back to the "fish swimming in water" notion. **If you were to track what you do in a week, you'd see the kind of knowledge you're wielding, often without even knowing it.** In one day you may be negotiating with renovation contractors on a better price and timeline, applying your knowledge of NBA coaching styles to managing your team, booking flights from your iPhone, making reservations at the new restaurant in town, roasting coffee in your garage, taking a course in the art of memoir, helping your brother set up his MacBook Pro, advising your neighbor on landscaping ideas, and telling your kids Greek mythology stories at

Everyone is a power broker ■

night. There are about a hundred little knowledge paths in that week that might lead you to talents worth tapping for both the delight and money. Start where you are.

DO YOU HAVE A SOUL SPECIALTY?

Here's how I define a soul specialty: It's a knack that you get off on. Scientific, I know.

I worked with Bobbi Jo in retail. We passed all of the pissed customers over to her.

"Crazy lady from Calgary wants her money back. Line two." Over to Bobbi. "Bring 'er on!" She couldn't wait to get her hands on the people whom the rest of us ran from: angry, disgruntled, sometimes certifiably loony, demanding patrons. Bobbi Jo's soul specialty was harmony. She wasn't out to get justice or make people right or wrong. Bobbi just really wanted everyone to jive—it was a positive obsession of hers. She created harmony everywhere. Her colors matched, she hummed all the time, she made mix CDs for presents, and she made sure the right people were sitting next to each other at the Christmas party. Her touch always smoothed things out. Soul knack.

WHAT'S YOUR MESSAGE?

Everyone has a message. What do you stand for? We could get really penetrating and esoteric about this. We could cowrite a tome on how to cull your values and such. But how about we just don't? Pretend it's an easy question.

What's your message? **What is it that you want people to know, see, understand, "get" in life?** What are you always mouthing off or preaching about? It could be as simple as "Freedom!" "Support the arts!" "Do unto others." You could borrow the bohemian credo: "Love, Truth, Beauty."

If you look closely, your message is showing up in everything you do in your life—or want to do with your life.

WHAT ARE THE VEHICLES FOR YOUR KNOWLEDGE?

How do you get heard? How do you disseminate your art and your message? Thanks to technology, the possibilities for communication are vast. You can blog it, tweet it, link it, post it to your Facebook page, or send it on its way via email chain. Where else do you show up? PTA meetings, the runner's clinic, advisory boards, your local pub. When you start to track all the routes to getting out there, you can start to home in on . . .

WHO WANTS WHAT YOU'VE GOT?

The answer to this is very rarely "everyone." There are two ways to approach this: Who shares your values, interests, and/or lifestyle aspirations? This is your tribe, your like-minded people. And second, who needs what you have to offer but doesn't know it yet? These are people you need to educate, convert, and invite into what you're offering.

Once you've looked at your industry and/or way of giving from some different angles, then it's good to examine your relationship to creativity and inspiration.

WHEN DOES YOUR MUSE VISIT YOU?

Call it what you want: the zone, the flow, the magical gap, the illuminating silence . . . there is a place in space and time where we tend to think and feel most clearly. And in that place is where *ahas*, creative sparks, strategies, and revelations flow our way.

Richard Bach, author of the metaphysical classic *The Bridge Across Forever,* called his muse the idea fairy, and she visited him when he was gardening or flying in a plane. He piloted his own Cessna and found his story lines among the clouds.

Certain conditions are more optimal for some people's muses than others: interaction, movement, nature, and contemplation. The trick is to find out what your muse loves the most and set the stage for her to enter. (Or him. Maybe your muse is of the male persuasion. I don't want to get any nasty letters from the Union of Muses for discrimination.)

Notice when and where ideas and solutions tend to enter your being. Maybe it's when you're talking to a particular friend or roaming the art gallery (interaction); when you're driving down the open highway or cycling to work (movement); walking among trees or napping on a dock (nature); or sitting in reflective silence or when the stereo is cranked and the lights are low (contemplation). Some people's idea fairies like to show up after a good meal or great sex, first thing in the morning, or just as they're drifting off to sleep.

DO RIGHT BY YOUR MUSE

Talk show host Charlie Rose asked folk rocker Neil Young about following his own muse. "So if you get an idea at, say, a dinner party, if you hear a tune or a lyric, do you excuse yourself from the party?" Charlie inquired.

"Of course. You never know when she'll [the muse] come again. I'm responsible to her." Sometimes, Neil would hide out in a bathroom to scratch out a song that was coming to him and return to his dinner guests after he felt he'd captured it.

When you feel an idea comin' on, excuse yourself. Pull over to the side of the road. Get lost in the creative flow. Be late. Barge in. Eccentricity makes muses especially horny.

Muses simply must be adored. They're as grandiose as they are generous. They like to be respected. If you meet them halfway, they'll give you the moon, the breakthrough concept, the stroke of . . . genius. Dis your muse and she's likely to stop dropping by. She's righteous. She likes to be appreciated. Genius is like that.

HAVE YOUR TOOLS READY

Master writer Anne Lamott keeps three-by-five white note cards and pens in every purse and drawer and vehicle to capture thoughts that float in as quickly as they float out. If I leave home without my Moleskine notebook and blue medium-point Paper Mate pen, I feel discombobulated, like I might miss my train. Keep a notepad by your nightstand. Leave yourself a voice mail. Don't assume that the best ideas will come back to you.

DO WHAT SHE TELLS YOU TO DO

She's busy, for sure, but the muse *loves* it when you actually play with her. When she drops an idea in your bucket you can push her to expound on what she's thinking. You can ask her what chapter should come next or where to look for funding. She could yammer till dawn and before you know it, you've mapped out your magnum opus.

Ignore your muse at your own peril. She doesn't always have it right, or maybe we don't always hear her clearly, but the more you heed her inspired wisdom, the faster you can drive on the Creative Awesomeness Highway. From idea to idea.

You and the muse in the diamond lane. Godspeed.

YOU'RE AN ARTIST, AND THAT'S THAT

Art making is not strictly about visual creations and producing material things. **Every single one of us is an artist—at something.** We lose ourselves in the creation of it; we're gifted at making it; we feel closer to ourselves and to a greater source when we do our art. The hairdresser who changes lives with just the right layering or shade of warm blonde is an artist. The facilitator who hears the meaning behind every question and weaves it all into a new vision for the whole group; the lover who senses just when to push you and when to let go; horse whisperers; baby whisperers; script doctors; troubleshooters; specialists; people who always get just the right gift; people who look you in the eye; and people who live fully in the moment itself.

When I say be creative, I don't mean you should all go and become great painters and great poets. I simply mean let your life be a painting, let your life be a poem.

—Osho

What "art" is and isn't is a cultural conversation that intellectuals love to gnaw on. What I want to raise here is the consideration that you can choose to be artful and poetic in anything and everything you do—especially in your work in the world. In the context of livelihood, I like Seth Godin's definition of art:

1. Art is made by a human being.
2. Art is created to have an impact—to change someone else.
3. Art is a gift. You can sell the souvenir, the canvas, the recording . . . but the idea itself is free, and the generosity is a critical part of making art.

Being artful is pouring your soul into it.
When we're giving our best, we're artistic.

When we're intentionally making something more beautiful, more understandable, more accessible, we're artistic.

When we reach below the surface and bring something thoughtful forward, we're being artistic. It's happening all of the time.

When you're bringing your whole self to the party, you're practicing your art form. Be it in conversation, on the canvas, or on the court, when you're creating something from your soul, you're making poetry happen.

"Life itself is a creative act," declares Patti Digh. "I see poetry everywhere—in the way a waiter hands me my vegan enchilada, in the way the train doors close at the Atlanta Hartsfield-Jackson International Airport, in the reflected smile of a cab driver in his rearview mirror when I ask about his children whose pictures are so proudly displayed." Patti is the author of *Life Is a Verb* and a diversity trainer. I attended a teleseminar of Patti's called "Playing with Your Creative Blocks," in which she posed this question:

If you knew that your art would support your life, how would you live? ■

That question climbed into me and set up camp. I meditated on it for two years. I printed it out in forty-point type and pasted it onto my notebooks. Before I planned any project, I went and sat with this question. Could I trust that my art would support my life? The only way to find out was to . . . trust, to operate from that place of luminous, fierce wishing within myself. I'd whisper the question repeatedly to myself and listen for the answers. Here's what showed up:

TO TRUST THAT YOUR ART WILL SUPPORT YOUR LIFE

Make creating art your guiding priority. Your vocation must revolve around making your art. Even if that means getting a job to subsidize making your art, set your life up so you have the space and resources to make your art. This is exactly why you must declare yourself an artist! You will need the mental fortitude to help you make the tough choices that come with prioritization, self-respect, and high standards. If it doesn't **contribute** to making your art, consider it an inconvenience.

Know that your life is content. Look at everything as material for your art. The inconveniences, the distractions—life—it all influences what you have to express and how you express it.

Create sacred physical and/or psychological space to make your art. This may be a corner in your bedroom with your laptop and an altar, a garage with an AM/FM radio, or an office with windows that open. "Space" could be your walk after dinner or the half hour you take in the morning to journal, a weekend in a motel with Wi-Fi, or a yearly silent retreat, unplugged so you can tune inward.

Invest in the best tools. A high-resolution computer monitor and ergonomic chair, membership associations, leading-edge conferences, well-cut clothes, the best cordless drill that money can buy. Take really good care of those tools. You can compromise on other stuff, but don't compromise on the essential gear that helps you to be great.

Work with the best people. Seek out people who are informed about their industry. Hire emerging superstars with natural talent or seasoned players with great track records. Collaborate with people who are impeccable with their word. Look for passion in others that matches yours in intensity. You're only as good as your team.

Continue your education. There are always new techniques to learn and developments to be aware of. Study other artists.

Believe that your art is going to be useful to someone. You don't really have a say in how or why your art will affect someone, but it will have an effect.

CRAFTING YOUR COMMERCE

Passion and paychecks isn't everyone's winning combination. For some of us, our soul's work has nothing to do with the employment that we choose. **It's entirely possible to have a purely practical job and find other outlets for your most precious gifts to be exercised.** I'm thinking about all the guys who work in factories and play in garage bands every weekend; the bookkeeper I know who is a galvanizing force for antiviolence campaigns in her community; and the legions of workers everywhere who do whatever it takes five days a week because they're passionate about making sure their kids have comfortable lives.

Some of us turn our art into actual careers. This can happen at any time, even right after we graduate from school—in which case, yay for you! You won the lottery of life destiny. Some of us are three professions into our work life when we finally discover what really lights our fire.

People who want to get paid for their passion have to answer some very practical questions. We have to migrate from the question of *What makes your soul shine most brightly?* to *How can you be consistently and increasingly excellent at it?* and *How can you profit from it?*

One of the best exercises for this is Jim Collins's Hedgehog Concept, from his now legendary book *Good to Great*. (Go to JimCollins.com and check out the audiovisual section for Jim's talk on this specifically.) When Collins was starting out his career he began keeping a journal about his personal and professional learning experiences. He likened this to a scientific study and approached himself as a specimen, "a bug called Jim." When he spent his day at work helping people understand computer networks, he noted: "Really enjoyed helping people understand the computers." He noticed that it wasn't the computing that excited him as much as it was the act of helping people to understand something. He logged the days when he worked on crunching data, and observed that he "loves making sense of data . . . the bug called Jim likes to teach." By observing these tangible self-discoveries from his life, Jim saw a framework emerge for success: What are you passionate about? What do you feel genetically encoded or born to do? And most simply, what can you make a living doing? According to Collins, it's how these three areas *intersect* that will determine your success. The sweet spot is the jackpot.

A VISUALIZATION FOR CREATION

Do what you need to do to quiet your mind. A cup of tea and ten deep breaths help.

PHASE 1: Imagine that you're in an empty room. It's your ideal room, so it could be plush and luxe, or austere and Zen. You love it and you're completely comfortable there.

Waiting outside the door to that room is your offering to the world. It could be your livelihood, a business, a product, a service, or a way you give love. How do you feel knowing that it's waiting for you outside the door? What is the flavor of your anticipation? (Anxious? Smiling? Dread? Blessed and blissful?)

Now, invite your business/product/service/artwork to join you. Do it ceremoniously or simply. Notice how you extend the invitation. (Sheepishly? Commanding? Open? Playfully? Hesitantly?) How does your business/product/service/artwork take form? As a ray of light, blueprint plans, a mighty robot, a peacock, a quivering beggar, a pile of gold, crates of best-selling books? How does your offering feel to you?

Just noticing how you extend the invitation and the form that your offering takes will be useful cosmic data. If you want to stop there, do so. Put the meditation on pause and come back to do Phase 2 another day.

Or, go further . . .

PHASE 2: Ask your business/product/service/artwork if it has a message or a gift to give you. Receive it. Notice how you receive it.

Ask your offering how it would like to be shared with the

world. You may hear or see specific strategies, or you may just feel the how—like feelings of integrity, innovation, steadiness.

Now (and this is important), let your offering enter into you. You can breathe it in, you can imagine opening your heart and letting it climb in, you can envision plugging into it and downloading it into your cells like an electrical current. The point: You and your business/product/service/artwork are entwined and grooving together—in unison.

Now glow. Radiate. Vibrate. Hum your sonic *powah,* baby. Envision your creative light making its way into the world effortlessly and being received with great appreciation. Allow the ease. Honor the excitement and intensity.

Say thank-you for what's on its way to you. Go meet it halfway.

WHAT BUSINESS ARE YOU REALLY IN?

W O R K S H E E T

What would someone pay you $100/hour to tell/teach/inform them about?

What are you repeatedly telling/showing/explaining to your clients? What do they want more of from you? What are they always asking for?

What do you know about? What's your knowledge base? What do you know that other people don't?

How does your service/offering/product make people feel? What problem does it solve, or what state does it create?

What's your message? (Everyone has a message.) What do you stand for?

What is the vehicle for your knowledge?

Who wants what you've got? (The answer to this is very rarely "everyone." There are two ways to approach this: values + lifestyle, and "types" of people.)

Who needs what you've got? (Even though they may not know it yet.)

promise character

image brand

persona style

personality offering

radiate integrity

reputation

real

SESSION 11

how you
show up
in the
world

Your genuine action will explain itself, and
will explain your other genuine actions.
Your conformity explains nothing.

—Ralph Waldo Emerson

If it looks good, you'll see it.
If it sounds good, you'll hear it.
If it's marketed right, you'll buy it.
But if it's true, you'll feel it.

—Kid Rock

If you're working in the marketing department of a major blue-chip firm crafting eco-friendly slogans to cover up your toxic waste, or at an ad agency devising sexy images about how cans of liquid sugar are going to make us feel groovy, then give me a minute of your time. If you're a solopreneur acting like you've got a big team on payroll, with offices on the top floor, when you're really just a one-person show rocking it out from your kitchen table, please pay attention to what I'm about to say. If your personal bio says things such as "Jane graduated at the top of her class and strives to pro-vide her customers with excellence"—if you're feeling even slightly closeted, cloaked, or hemmed in by your own professional image, listen up.

YEP, YOU'RE A BRAND

"Listen, lady, I'm a carpenter in a small town. I'm not a brand, I'm a woodworker. Been doing what I do for fifteen years because I love it. And if you think human beings are brands, then what's the world coming to?"

This is what happens when you go on national television and preach about personal branding, like I did one night. Someone's going to get all ruffled, thinking that you want people to Photoshop their lives and start talking like cereal ads. Au contraire. Yes, I want you to have gleaming white teeth and a great cocktail line so that you can be an opportunity magnet. **But this is about soul packaging, not persona manufacturing.** And yes, Carpenter Joe, you are, and always have been, *a brand*.

The term *branding* is problematic because it evokes commercial associations. Name brands, brands of toothpaste, "Do you carry that brand?" It's all very department store and Wonder bread. Those are product types. We're here to talk about personal brands. **You. You at work. You in the world. You.**

Elizabeth Talerman is the founder of Nucleus, a brand strategy collaborative in New York. They're a hip and reputable agency, and you've probably watched, drunk, or driven one of the products of Elizabeth's many clients. I love her definition of a brand (you can exchange the word *person* for *organization*): "Inside every organization is a driving force, a sense of purpose. This force is your brand. It is what you stand for. It is what sets you apart. It's not a slogan or an ad campaign. It's a living thing—the net result of behavior."

Schoolteachers, government workers, soccer coaches, home security services, an organic tea company, a carpet-laying business: Every person and service has its own quality of character, based on how it shows up in the world. "For big companies with product development operations," Elizabeth says, "and for an individual, it starts with integrity, authenticity, a clear and consistent message, and a **true understanding of what you do in the world that is of benefit to others.** Whether we're talking about a massive Fortune 500 brand or an individual, it's all the same."

Do you really love what you love?
Are you who you say you are?
Who are you, anyway?

Your character, your brand, informs your image—not the other way around. This is where the concept of branding can go very wrong. It's not about contriving an image that you hope will sell or be accepted. That's what the managers of boy bands do. That's what a lot of us do at speed-dating parties and with boilerplate résumés. Branding yourself with respect to your livelihood is about getting clear on your attributes, **identifying which of those attributes is most vital to your success,** and defining what you then offer to the world as a result of those attributes.

Again, this works for individuals just like it does for companies. Your brand is your character in action. It's what you build your reputation on. It's what you're known for. What would your customers or coworkers say about you? That's how they perceive your brand.

Building "trustworthy" brands with integrity is the conversation du jour because so many of us have forgotten how to trust ourselves—and one another. Understandably. You never know if someone's face is her real face, if reality TV is reality, or if a celebrity's tweet "just had the best burger at Carl's!" is genuine or a paid covert endorsement.

And then, of course, we have our own age-old conundrum of fitting in and standing out. It's the divine dilemma of simultaneously wanting to be unique and profoundly wanting to belong. That will never change. On top of that deep driving psychology, we pile on social norms such as dress codes and executive titles, salary structures, and trying to throw perfect patio parties like those pastel-colored people in home style magazines do. And then there's the popularity contest that is social media itself, and, well . . . it's the makings of an identity crisis.

And let us not forget about the plethora of popular experts that publishers love to publish and we love to consume. (Insert sheepish grin.) We're always scanning for the best new advice from the leading edge of the best new smart people. (Insert batting eyelashes. Blink wink.)

If you can tune out the noise of "how-to" and "ten steps" and "proven tactics," you will be able to hear your own Spidey sense—genuine, sincere intuition—and it will tell you that . . .

You are the expert on you ■

INTEGRITY BRANDS, CHARACTER, AND REAL PERSONAS

Always be a first-rate version of yourself, instead of a second-rate version of somebody else.

—Judy Garland

Acting like something you're not is not only emotionally, spiritually, and frequently financially exhausting, it's unsustainable. **Image is a fragile thing.** Sincerity is rock solid.

Here's what brands with integrity and true characters know for sure:

TRANSPARENCY IS SEXY

Care more about being accurately, precisely who you are than caring what anyone might think about you. Be daring enough to tell us—your customers, your fans, your people—about your ambitions because we'll be the ones to help you fulfill them.

Expect to offend some people. If you're not having some polarizing effects, then you're not fully showing up.

ONLY THE SELF-REFERENCING THRIVE

The starting point is *Who am I?* not *What will sell?* Your foundation has to be built on your real passion. The rest of branding is about accurate packaging.

CONSISTENCY WINS

Keep on being yourself, relentlessly. We can count on Apple to innovate. We know that Ford trucks will always be tough. We could rely on Dr. Martin Luther King, Jr., to deliver his vision with strength. Being consistent doesn't mean you don't change or evolve. Look at Madonna. She's consistently reinventing herself. Reinvention *is* her brand. When you consistently and genuinely show up, you build trust.

PRIDE IS POSITIVE

Rejoice and love yourself today
'Cause baby, you were born this way.

—Lady Gaga

I have never met someone who is living a bold and success-ful life—and by *successful* I mean prosperous, kind, and in touch with the meaningfulness of what he's doing—who has apologized for being perfectionistic, mercurial, unrelenting, or whatever his slightly controversial hallmark characteristics are. You will always be too much of something for someone: too big, too loud, too soft, too edgy. If you round out your edges, you lose your edge.

EMOTIONS ARE MAGNETIC

Emotional labor is available to all of us,
but it is rarely exploited as a competitive
advantage.

—Seth Godin

If you don't emote, you're remote. Emotion is the chemistry of resonance. People, clients, customers, and audiences say *Yes!* when they can relate to your vibration.

True character is having the courage to defy your position and express your emotions. We stand up and say things. We lean forward. We risk. We laugh out loud, show our true colors, and speak our minds. We make declarations.

We are charming. We're not charming to everyone, of course. Not everyone is going to fall for our shtick or want to buy our goodies. But we'll charm the people who relate to us. And you know what that is? That's love.

STUDY YOURSELF

If you tell a true story, you can't be wrong.

—Jack Kerouac

HEAR YOUR OWN STORY

We may sporadically get asked some penetrating questions throughout our lives, but most of us rarely have the opportunity to be the subject of a focused interview. Having the honor of being in that hot seat can be incredibly illuminating, and it's an effective way to clarify your driving force and what defines you.

Get interviewed. Have you got a staff meeting? A job interview? A thesis to defend? A team to lead? A business to run? Children to teach? A lover to love? Are you planning on leaving the house this year? Good. Then this assignment applies to you: Get interviewed about why you do what you do in the world.

Find a writer—someone with the listening skills to pry and evoke your best stories and intelligence from you. Can't afford a writer? Ask a friend to interview you. Hell, interview yourself! Channel your inner Barbara Walters. Pretend that no one is listening, or pretend you have a rapt audience of millions.

Here's why: **When you are properly interviewed, you will hear things that you didn't hear about yourself before.** You'll let it flow from your depths and the heights. You'll think harder. You'll surprise yourself.

Get it on video. When you see yourself on tape, you will laugh, cringe, and swell with assuring confidence. Consider it cheap media training. You'll notice how many times you say "Um, uh, well . . . " You'll notice your body language—when you slouch (fear), when you get animated (strength), when your breathing flows (inspiration), and when it doesn't.

You'll capture content! If you ramble for twenty minutes about you and your business, it's almost guaranteed that you'll say one zinger line that turns out to be your slogan or new mantra. And in your rambling and riffing and storytelling, you may hear a manifesto or a new magic formula. Project ideas will leap to the surface. Your blog copy or next speech will appear. New names and connections will start to spark.

Seeing yourself on film can be one of the most cringe-eliciting or touching experiences. I highly recommend it. Yep, I'm talking to you. All of you. You with the webcam that you've never used. All you camera-shy folks. You with no particular reason to be on film. You can use it for posterity's sake or as brand refinement. You can file it under *time capsule, obituary,* or *love letter,* or consider it training for when your fifteen minutes of fame strikes.

LEVERAGE YOUR SO-CALLED SHORTCOMINGS

Disclaimer: The following theory does not apply to heart surgeons, shrinks, or pharmacists. Or engineers who build bridges.

Being formally qualified is overrated. Passion and results can be the best credentials there are. When we try to hide our lack of qualifications we actually weaken the potential strength of our brand.

Bill Gates, Richard Branson, Steve Jobs. All billionaires. All college dropouts. Jimi Hendrix couldn't read music. Rachael Ray never went to cooking school. John Fluevog went from working in a shoe store to creating his own shoe empire. Vera Wang was a fashion writer. Coco Chanel had no formal training.

I myself am the poster chick for unqualified. The only time I've spent inside a college was when I was in diapers. My mother, eighteen when she had me, took me to school with her so she could complete her degree in social studies. I doodled in psych textbooks and played with my dollies at the back of the classroom. You could say I got my BA by osmosis. To be clear: I *juuust* made it to the right side of the tracks, and then I ran like hell . . . straight into great jobs and wrangling a staff of PhDs.

And then there's Stella. Stella is an interior decorator who's been in the business for more than a decade. She had a thriving design firm and accolades out the wazoo. And yet, she still felt a niggling need to go to school to get certified.

"Why would you want to waste your time doing that?" I asked. "You have a waiting list for your clients."

"Well, I'd feel more legit," she said.

"You made more than a hundred grand last year and your clients refer you all the time. Isn't that legit?" I asked. She was resisting, so I ramped up my persisting. "You know what you should say in your bio?" I said to her. "Say that you're self-taught, in eighteen-point bold type. Let people know that you never set foot in a design college because you were too busy sewing your own drapes, shopping for textiles with your grandma, and learning how to build cabinets after school with your dad. It's in your blood. Self-taught says 'extra amazing.' Self-taught says 'natural talent.' Just come out with it."

She skipped school.

FOR BUSINESS

For the love of God and the information highway, please write your bio in first person—we all know you wrote it anyway. One of the most highly trafficked pages on small business websites is the "About" page. People are hiring you, paying attention to you, coming to see you. So they want to hear from . . . *you.*

IDENTIFY THE BIG REAL
OF WHAT YOU'RE DOING

Strong personal branding always goes back to the root of your purpose. Do you know the story about the two stonecutters? When asked what he was doing, the first man replied, "I'm cutting this stone into bricks." When the second laborer was asked the same question, he replied, "I'm building a cathedral."

How much do we do in a day with our nose to the grindstone? Myopic, focused, making a list and checking it twice. Done. Done. And done. But what are we really up to?

There is a Big Real behind everything we do. Sometimes it's a negative Big Real: You're wasting your life in that low-paying nine-to-five job. Sometimes it's a positive Big Real: You're touching people's lives in that low-paying nine-to-five job.

BIG REAL REFRAMES

Working overtime again? How about: You're making sure you can get to Miami for your next holiday to flame your mojo?

Hauling your ass out of bed for a run? How about: You're connecting with the power of your body and tapping into your creative spirit?

Cutting people's hair? How about: Your salon is a place where people heal and have both their inner and outer beauty witnessed?

Waiting on tables? How about: You're learning and teaching loving-kindness?

Look up. Zoom out from the daily tasks and see the holy weaving of your time and love and action. Being conscious of the true meaning of your work will buoy you in both the seemingly trivial and the seemingly impossible tasks of your work.

KNOW YOUR INFLUENCES

If you've ever asked yourself, *What would so-and-so do?* then that person is an influence for you. Your intellectual and spiritual influences show up in your big decisions, in the ideas you love so much that you wish you'd thought of them, and in the goals you aim for. Your influences can come from within your industry, or they can come from outlying, totally unrelated sources.

In his book *Do More Great Work,* Michael Bungay Stanier offers the best influences exercise I've come across. He's been kind enough to throw it into our fire:

WHO'S GREAT?

Think of eight heroes—role models you think are inspiring for one reason or another. They can be famous or not (George Clooney, your mother), real or not (Queen Elizabeth, Buzz Lightyear), alive or not (Desmond Tutu, Gandhi). Scan your world, and think about people whose stories capture your imagination—folks you've always held in high esteem, who embody something you think is impressive. You might even be a bit envious of them. (I know, eight is a lot. But stick with it.)

The role models don't even have to be people. If it resonates with you, a hero could be an object that you admire or that sparks your imagination (the MINI Cooper or a Ford truck) or even a company or organization that you think does great work (Apple or Greenpeace or Google).

Narrow that list to five. Choose the five you feel are the most compelling, about whom you'd be most likely to say *Yes, I'd like to embody what they've got*. For each hero, list four characteristics that are inspiring to you. These can be behaviors, qualities you sense, or situations they have created.

Look for patterns in your lineup of role models. Recurring themes or words can give you a clue about what you believe is important, how you'd like to behave, and where seeds of your own Great Work might lie.

IT'S ALL SELF-PROMOTION, BABY

The market for something to believe in is infinite.

—Hugh MacLeod, *Ignore Everybody*

Your voice mail, your email signature line, your business card, the personalized note that you tuck in, how you introduce yourself to the receptionist, what you wear, the tip you leave, the thank-you cards you send—it's all public relations and branding. **You are constantly sending a signal to the world. And the world responds accordingly.**

My dear friend Chris Guillebeau set a goal for himself to visit every country on the planet before his thirty-fifth birthday. Slacker, eh? He started *ArtofNonConformity.com* community, wrote a book similarly titled, and has tens of thousands of people following his journey and learning from his lessons. He's the Gentleman of the Internet and a master at nonslimy self-promotion.

"It's the difference between evangelism and recruitment," says Chris. "Evangelism is like a vacuum cleaner salesman going out and knocking on two hundred doors a day. By the end of the day you might sell one vacuum, but you've had one hundred and ninety-nine rejections."

In short, it's a total pain in the ass and you have to deal with rejection all the time. "That's evangelism. Whereas recruitment—or what I think of as self-promotion—is more about finding a tribe and going out and saying, 'Here's what I'm doing. I'm inviting people to be a part of this. Here's what it's all about: the mission and the vision. If you identify with this, I'd love to have you be a part of it. If it's not the right thing for you, then go and have fun, do your own thing, and that's great.'"

Chris's final tips: "Don't call it marketing. Connect with one person at a time. Start with who you know."

THE TOP REASONS PEOPLE HATE SELF-PROMOTION, AND WHY THEY NEED TO JUST GET OVER IT

"It makes me feel like I'm pushing something on someone." Passion is a force—and an essential one at that. If you're not enthusiastic about what you're offering, you shouldn't be offering it in the first place. If you're not passionate, you have to fake it, and that'll just make you feel like a sleazeball. Do you want to be a passionflower or a wallflower?

"But I'm shy." You have three choices here:

1. Get over it. There's nothing like the necessity of putting food on the table or the drive to achieve your life dreams to cure shyness. Successful people do it all the time.
2. Let someone else do the selling for you—a writer, a rep, an agent, a virtual assistant type.
3. Pray that opportunity will knock on your door. This tactic, on its own, never ever works.

"But it's not a talent of mine." See the previous entry. Get over it.

"But I'm afraid that people will think less of me. That I'll be seen as less of an artist, social steward, or a true professional if I'm hawking my wares or blowing my own horn." You think Picasso wasn't actively promoting his artwork when he sat in the front row of the bullfights for everyone to see? Or that Steve Jobs wasn't reinforcing his personal brand by wearing that same damn black mock turtleneck and those Levis all the time? Do you think all the power bloggers are tweeting all the time just to be of service to the unified Twittersphere of love? Artists sell.

PRO.MO'

So here's where to start with it all. Anchor into this reality and truth: You are offering the world something that you wholeheartedly believe in. Repeat: You're anchored, with integrity, to purpose and meaning. That being the case, and the premise for everything I'm about to say, let's proceed with passion-based, values-driven, do-good-things-in-the-world, unabashedly proud self-promotion.

Don't burn too much energy trying to assume how people will perceive you. What some people will read as enthusiastic stamina, others will interpret as pushy intrusion. (This is not something you'll hear in marketing class.) It's your job to show up as you, passion and all, and let the right customers make up their mind about you.

Go for the low-hanging fruit. Who already loves you, baby? When you're setting out to promote or sell yourself, just start where the love is. It's so much easier that way—and easy is efficient. Go to your existing clients and customers. Go to your friends and family. Sell them. Ask them to talk you up, refer you, bring friends to your opening party, or give you a testimonial. . . .

Up-sell them. Ask them what they love about your product or service. Ask them what they want more of from you—and listen to them. Develop upgrades, exclusivity, deeper programs, add-ons, advanced courses, communities. Give them kickbacks; share the wealth. Ask them what dream they would dream for you.

Competition. Who is your so-called competition? Who's in your industry? For instance: You're a business coach—business is your specialty. Who are the relationship or creativity coaches that you respect and admire? How could you team with them to create an event, offering, product, or program?

Radiate your passion + clearly state the facts of what that passion generates = happy self-promotion ■

When you collaborate, you enrich creative thinking, you gain access to someone else's resources, you create an immediate referral system, and you get to give—which always makes you stronger. If you do it out of expediency or usury, it never works. The key to successful collaborations is respect, admiration, and the intention that you'll make something better together than you would apart.

Use what you've got from day one. At the start of a venture, sometimes all you have to sell is passion and promise. You haven't proven your business model; you have no customers; you're new on the block. All you've got is *Step Right Up!* hoopla. And sometimes, that's enough.

If you love what you do and believe that it's going to make a positive difference in people's lives—whether it's your wedding photography, your coaching methodology, your end-cancer campaign, or your gadget invention—then you, my friend, are ahead of the game. You're light-years down the path from the sorry sods who don't even dare to dream.

THE ALL-ABOUT-YOU
INTERVIEW
W O R K S H E E T

Arm the best-known listener in your life, a professional copywriter, or your very own talented self with these prompts for storytelling and philosophical insight.

1. What do you know to be true, unquestionably beyond doubt, certain with every cell of your being, completely, passionately, righteously certain?

2. What was the dumbest thing that you used to believe in? What changed your mind?

3. What do you know the most about?

4. Why do you do what you do?

5. One word: *breakthrough*. What comes to mind?

6. What has been one of your most memorable experiences in your career?

7. What global policy, credo, practice, or law would you like to decree?

8. What experience tested your mettle but made you a better person?

9. Finish this sentence: "It's a good day when . . . "

10. When was the last time you thought, "Yes! That person has so got it going on!"?

11. What question in your life has had the biggest impact on you?

continues on next page

12. What are you positively addicted to? (Psych 101 defines positive addiction as "a healthy high that makes you stronger." As long as the craving for it doesn't take you over, then it's, like, totally cool.)
13. What's the best advice you were ever given in terms of business?
14. What's the most common life advice that you give to your friends?
15. What's the first thing that comes to mind when you hear the word *devotion*?
16. What are you most interested in?
17. What are you incredibly grateful for?
18. What's your form of service to the world?

THE ASK-A-FRIEND SURVEY

W O R K S H E E T

Oh would some power the gift give us,
to see ourselves as others see us!

—Robert Burns

Asking someone who cares about you how they actually perceive you is courageous. It's the kind of vulnerability that could crack you open. Sometimes another perspective can create a quantum leap for us. So take a deep breath and just ask.

The prerequisite is this: Send these questions (or make up your own) only to someone whom you respect, who makes you feel more like yourself, and who actively adores you. This isn't about being critiqued or toughened up. The purpose of this exercise is to see yourself more clearly so that you can rise to your own fullness.

Dear Friend,

I'm taking a leap. Reaching out. Trolling for insights, reflections, and objectivity . . . from you so that I can see myself more clearly.

1. What do you think is my greatest strength?
2. How would you describe my style of living?
3. What do you think I should let go of?
4. When do you feel that I am at my best?
5. What do you wish I were less of, for my sake?
6. When have you seen me really shine?
7. What do you think I could give myself more credit for or celebrate more?

freedom

flexibility lifestyle

liberty days

seasons space

intentional direction

SESSION 12

calling all sovereigns of time!

In the name of the Fire,
The Flame
And the Light;
Praise the pure presence of fire
That burns from within
Without thought of time.

—John O'Donohue, poet

The only reason for time is so that
everything doesn't happen at once.

—Albert Einstein

TIME DIETS + STARVING SPIRITS

I've tried many a time management system: Focus days, buffer days. An emptied in-box, flagged emails. Restrained meandering. Timed phone calls. No phone calls. Quadrants. Categories. Categorizing my life into quadrants of ambition and lists of goals divided by the square root of how many productive milliseconds I could squeeze out of any given day—at least five days a week, but with time off for religious holidays. Alas, time was still the boss of me. And a nasty one, at that.

Systems for running our lives can be useful, but they can also enslave us. Time management can be the biggest trap of them all. It can creep into your psyche, and rather than freeing you up, it's calling all the shots.

Time management can be a lot like dieting. We portion out our time, like food, so we have optimal energy and results. Diets help us lose unwanted weight. Time management systems help us lose unwanted tasks. Diets focus our food intake so we can shed pounds and be freer in our bodies. Time management focuses our task intake so we can shed hubristic to-dos and be freer in our days.

And . . . most diets don't work to keep the weight off. Same goes for time diets, but their failing is more difficult to spot. It's much more insidious. How do you know a time management system isn't working for you? Well, there's the obvious sign that you're not getting done what you want to get done, or it's too complicated to maintain so you quit it. But there is a subtler, more critical indicator: a hovering feeling that you answer to someone else. You feel like time is a boss that you need to please, and that you labor for time—the better you perform, the more time you get given.

If you believed in Santa Claus when you were a kid, you might recall that *Santa is coming!* anticipation that was one part thrilling and two parts terror. That anxiety you had every December that if you stepped out of line, your Easy-Bake Oven or G.I. Joe wasn't going to show up under the tree, because Santa Claus was tracking your every childish move. Grown-ups don't have Father Christmas issues anymore; we have Father Time issues—conflict with an imagined authority that doles out rewards for our good behavior.

Does this sound familiar? The thought of having an unstructured day, even if it's on vacation, makes you break out in hives. Calling friends becomes part of your quarterly objectives. You feel guilty for taking time off from work to relax or play—"work" can be anything from your day job to cutting the lawn on the weekend. You schedule in spontaneity. You complete a task that wasn't on your to-do list, but you write it on your to-do list anyway just so you can have the satisfaction of crossing it out. Time management could be managing you.

Some people diet obsessively. Some people manage their time obsessively. Both obsessions can be driven by a lack of self-worth—a constant striving to be more acceptable, more productive . . . better. **Time management systems can suppress our own innate wisdom and cravings for vitality.** Your calendar may say it's a "high-priority day" when really, you need a break to reconnect with your mom or cook a good meal, very slowly. You block out two hours to work on your project plan, but then your best friend's telephone number shows up on the caller ID and you're faced with an immediate conflict. You push yourself when your heart isn't in it. Your to-do list becomes more important than your fatigue. You work to earn your time off, and you're too beat to enjoy it when you get it.

Socially speaking, we may be productive and on schedule, but we're not any less stressed or more fulfilled. We're obsessed with the doing of life, adrift from the being.

In *Women, Food, and God,* Geneen Roth peels back the layers: "Freedom from obsession is not about something you do: It's about knowing who you are. It's about recognizing what sustains and exhausts you." So if we're going to kick our time diets, then everything that gets on our calendar needs to be assessed for its nutritional value. The guiding question becomes *Does this sustain me or exhaust me?*

Time regimes can certainly do wonders for getting the most out of life. We need them, like we need good eating habits. I batch my actionable tasks, I schedule in administrivia days, and I have key priorities, because accomplishing a lot is a major rush for me. But it's my relationship to those time management methodologies that makes all the difference in my psyche and therefore the quality of what I do.

I shifted how and why I use productivity tools.

TYRANT TIME	POWER TIME
Quantity driven. Uses time management systems to crank out lots and lots and lots of stuff.	**Quality focused.** Uses time systems to create *space and freedom*—which then allows you to make more meaningful, substantive things.
Competitive. Compares your productivity with how productive everyone else is.	**Self-referencing.** What matters is what you're doing that is of value.
Time is in charge. Free time is something you earn. Time is dispensed to you.	**I'm in charge.** Things need to earn your time and attention. *You* are the dispenser of time.
Transactional. You put in time, you get time back.	**Relational.** If you relate with the moment—if you're present—there is a giving and a receiving that happens simultaneously.
Logical. Time is measured only by the clock.	**Magical.** Time can be expanded and contracted by energy. With pure intention, you can accomplish a day's work in an hour, you can get an hour's worth of rest in a moment of contemplation, and you can make big things happen very quickly.

When you're clear on what activates the joy within you, time management becomes a means to self-expression, not self-policing. And "making time" becomes an act of service so that you can be your best for those around you.

It all depends on how you approach your relationship with time: . . . as a soldier or a dancer; as obedient or visionary. Time is here to serve *you*.

TIME PERSONALITIES

Quit thinking time is "out there." Take ownership of time—acknowledge that you are where it comes from—and it will stop owning you. Claim time as yours and it will release its claim on you.

—Gay Hendricks

Gay Hendricks wrote an excellent book about overcoming barriers to happiness called *The Big Leap,* in which he builds the case that a major cause of discontent and angst is a screwed-up relationship with time. Just like many of us adopt personas to navigate through public life—the Peace Keeper, the Shy Kid, the Party Girl—Hendricks figures that we also have time personas that rule our schedules and habits. He offers:

- **The Time Cop** (if you count the minutes, you'll always be on time), and
- **The Time Slacker** ("What's the problem? I'm only five minutes late") as two examples. I'll add some character types to the tickle trunk. . . .

I'll add to the list of time characters with:

- **Time Hackers** aspire for "the four-hour workweek." They outsource as much as they can in their lifestyle and build boundaries around their availability so that they have plenty of time to play.
- **Time Benders** take a more wizardly approach. They believe, like Einstein did, that time is a construct of the mind, and so a fluid and abundant mind-set creates an abundant experience of time. You accomplish more in less time. In this headspace, synchronicity plays a part in productivity, and trust in the abundance of life keeps you focused on the finish line.

Each time persona has its strengths and weaknesses. You can get psychoanalytical about why you've been molded into a certain character, but what's most important for our liberation mission is that you're aware that you can change your time persona. You can refuse to rush and still arrive on time; you can have all the energy you need to accomplish what you want and not be fried when you're finished; you can find some grace in the less pleasurable must-dos, and you can **fill your days doing what you love with people you cherish.**

Whatever is

on your plate

got there because

you said yes

to it ■

WE KNOW YOU'RE BUSY.
NOW SHUT UP ABOUT IT.

So sorry, I've been busy. I'm just so busy with . . . I've been too busy to . . .

Busy? Get in line. That's life. That's my life. That's most people's lives. Grown-up humans tend to be . . . busy. Add kids, jobs, or curveballs to the mix and you have all that much more of life to be busy about.

"I'm so busy." A contemporary anthem. A typically hurried, whiny refrain that doesn't make us look more important or productive; rather, it reinforces the victim mentality that doing, doing, doing is our duty, damn it.

Sometimes we take on to-dos and commit to climb mountains because our soul is called to. Sometimes life throttles us with unforeseen and unrelenting demands, such as growing families and aging parents and fledgling businesses. Busy can be great. Busy can suck. But most often, busy is a choice.

I don't buy the "busier than our predecessors / age of technology / workaholic culture" argument. Yes, we appear to be more compulsive, less nuclear, and able to survive on less sleep than everyone in *Little House on the Prairie,* but their lives were just as packed, planting potatoes and raising barns, surviving from sunup to sundown. Before microwaves and disposable diapers and Internet access, our grannies worked to keep it all humming.

We fill up our lives. That's what humans do. The question is what are you filling it with? Are you out-of-control busy, or are you full with life? Full is beautiful. Frantic is a buzz kill.

Changing how you speak about your time affects your relationship with it. It's the power of positive time talk. So what do you tell 'em when you can't fit another moment into your day-timer, when you have to send regrets, or have to pass on a sweet opportunity? Tell them the truth. Report on life, rather than whining about it. *My family needs me this week. I've got my head down for this deadline. I've got to pull back.* **Let people meet you in your clear truth rather than your apologetic panic.** *I've got lots on the go but I'm happier than ever. I want to spend more time with my kids so I'm cutting back my hours. The accident slowed me down—it's been a blessing and a curse. My family will be visiting so I'd like to push back the deadline.* And sometimes—many times—you don't need to excuse yourself at all. Just show up. Present and accountable, full of life and its demands. We all understand.

WHAT MATTERS MOST

From a leaflet in the entry of a Benedictine monastery that I adore: "Above all, prayer holds the first place in the monk's day and nothing must be preferred to this activity. Prayer involves coming into contact with divine life, in openness to the mystery of love which is written in our hearts."

The monks are encouraged to stop their chores if they feel inspired to pray. The longing to pray comes before work and all other tasks. The brothers pray seven times a day in collective chanting and in solitude. True, most monks needn't worry about organizing staff parties, their wardrobe stress is nil, and they're not juggling Junior's soccer practice and piano lessons. **But the optimal concept here is passion coming before tasks.** It doesn't matter whether you're living off the grid or high on the hog; devotion requires . . . devotion.

How many mornings do we choose email over meditation, or let deadlines pull rank on stretching, cuddling, or a glass of water swallowed slowly and appreciated? How habitually do we override the call from the interior of our being? The call to pray, or listen, or just to be fully awake in noticing what is being said to us—whether it's our heart, the dog, the trees, or our fellow humans speaking to us?

Have mercy.

Keep them safe.

How lovely.

Courage, please.

I need you.

I love you.

Thank you.

Yes.

Prayer comes in all forms and every one spoken brings grace to the day. Our hearts are the altars. Each day lived is another chance to reap the deep rewards of sacred prioritization. Attend first to the divine and the work at hand becomes art.

A PERFECT TWELVE

WORKSHEET

In Esther and Jerry Hicks's book *Ask and It Is Given,* Abraham Hicks suggests a beautiful exercise whereby you **envision your ideal twelve hours.**

I'd like to add a twist to that: Envision an ideal "Home Day" (a slightly more down-to-earth scenario) and an ideal "Away Day" (a more fantastical scenario). It's important to imagine both a doable day and a fantastical day because we want to create images that feel resonant and reachable, and loosen up some bigger possibility thinking.

HOME DAY PERFECTION

Keep your vision within the confines of space and time. Let your imagination and idealism unfurl, but save grossly impractical things like, "I wake up in Athens, lunch in Manhattan, and smoke a bedtime hookah in Rajasthan," for your Away Day fantasy.

In everyday life, where would you be, what would you be doing, who would you be with, what would you be eating, how would you be earning, helping, creating, living, loving *in a span of twelve hours*? Walk through everything that would go into the waking hours of blissdom for you.

Focus on ideal. If bliss would be "I'm working in my jammies from home," and presently you're commuting three hours to the office, write it down anyway.

AWAY DAY PERFECTION

In an extravagant or time-bending day, where would you be, what would you be doing, whom would you be with, what would you be eating, how would you be earning, helping, creating, living, loving *in a span of twelve hours*?

The whole point of this exercise is to actually create those ideal twelve hours—or as close to it, even if it's just fifteen minutes, as frequently as possible until that idealism is the fabric of your everyday reality and lifestyle. Day to day makes up a lifetime.

generous cash

gain fortune

prospering ease

give plenty

treasure wealth

abundant

SESSION 13

money:
more
is more.
enough
is plenty.

Money is only a tool. It will take you wherever you wish, but it will not replace you as the driver.

—Ayn Rand

WHAT DO YOU NEED MONEY FOR?

In terms of physical existence, there are two kinds of having: the material and the experiential. Stuff to own, keep, borrow; and experiences to *experience*. The question is, what actually matters to you? Where does your money meet the meaningfulness of your life?

Beyond the basics of food, shelter, and health, what do you need money for? Does beauty matter? Does comfort matter? Does stability have great meaning for you, or the capacity to travel the world? If you say it matters to you, then it matters. And what matters varies wildly from person to person.

You are
the economist
of what matters
to you ■

Luxury might be a necessity for your peace of mind. Tithing may be part of your basics. Freedom could mean stock options and a company expense account, or it could be the liberty to design your own day, every day. Culture could be owning a Francesco Clemente portrait, or having enough money after you pay bills to buy a round at the pub. You could use your disposable income to shop organic or to fund an expedition to Everest.

When you establish your purpose for money, you have a rudder to help guide your purchases, investments, donations, savings—all the things that you do with money. You also motivate yourself to go get what you want the most.

Tucked into my planner is a tattered and love-worn list titled "My Purpose for Money." When I wrote it I was living hand to mouth, had just been rejected by an art school, and was officially lost—it was the perfect time to steady my aim. Every single word in my purpose list is intentional and prayer soaked. And because of that, the list has just as much relevance ten years later. I'm a ways from fulfilling my purpose for money, but in varying degrees, I'm on the right path.

Do you want to make a million bucks a year? Why? For what? Do you really need it to do what you want to do and be who you want to be this lifetime, or do you need more? How much will be enough if you've reached your lifestyle goals? And who really needs "more than enough"?

Conscious wealth has greater value.

MY PURPOSE FOR MONEY

Rapidly create a lasting empire of hip-consciousness products + writings . . . beautiful communication.

Travel with Scott, our child, friends and family, widely and freely.

Create and invest in socially responsible ventures.

Generously and frequently gift family and friends.

Be a philanthropist.

Own a beautiful home in Vancouver.

Spend time in a luxury space in Santa Fe (and elsewhere . . .)

Buy beautiful art.

Get clear on your desired life. Then you'll be clear on your purpose for money. Then you can match your purpose with your actions. This is the heart of lifestyle design. (I highly recommend Tim Ferriss's "dreamlining" exercise in *The 4-Hour Workweek* book. It's posted on his website for free. He offers a formula that's just the right combination of visionary and nitty-gritty and, in his words, "reverses the repression" of being on the hamster wheel of earning and spending. Go get it.)

Money enables so many of our wants to be manifested. The clearer we are on those wants, the freer we are from the mind-sets and social systems that inspire both greed and limited thinking. In analyzing the full spectrum of your money needs, you may realize that your ideal lifestyle is much simpler than you believed, or that you're more ambitious than you thought you were.

Bend your paradigm.

Let the money follow the meaning.

THE VALUE OF VALUE

Accolades. Salary. Grades. Titles. Holding the door, being heard, singing our praises, taking our feelings into account, good manners. **R-E-S-P-E-C-T.** Everybody wants it.

The world reflects back to you how much you value yourself. It's a law. Granted, it's a slightly mutable law. Because once in a while someone will come along as we're muddling with esteem and dreams and point out how golden we are. They'll treat us with the kind of respect that stops us in our mucky tracks. Those people are angels, and they are everywhere. (You're likely one of them. You do that for people and might not even know it.) A weak handshake sets the tone. You're sheepish with your new employer and they start you off in the lowest salary bracket. You don't value your time so you think it's okay that your friend always keeps you waiting. People who believe that they bring something to the table no matter where they are have an aura about them. They can be affable or assertive, but they command a reciprocity of respect for their personal space and their time.

At the end of the day, if we don't value ourselves, what can we expect from anyone else?

Worthiness is such tender terrain.

A NOD TO THOSE WITH THE ENTREPRENEURIAL SPIRIT

Sales solve everything.

> —Mark Cuban

The question I get asked the most in terms of money-making and priorities is about what to focus on first. Here's the only mantra you need: **Get the money in the door.** That's it. I see too many people worrying about getting their business cards printed, or being "ready" for the sales rush, that they forget the whole point of the first few years of business: *survive*.

FIRST: DO WHAT MAKES YOU THE MOST MONEY, *THE FASTEST*

What can you do in your business to make money *right now*? Today? This week? And the week after that? Do it. I'll bet you it doesn't rely on having the perfect logo or the right suit to wear. You might even be able to get the cash moving without having a website and by just picking up the phone. Let me recap: No money, no business. Go get the money.

SECOND: DO WHAT MAKES YOU THE *MOST* MONEY

The fast money may not be the big money. But you need to make time to work on the big money-making projects, though they tend to take longer to manifest.

For the first year of a start-up or a new project, you might want to spend about two-thirds of your time focused on the revenue streams that will allow you to survive and move toward thriving.

At the same time—and this is why the hours can get *ca-ra-zeee*—you need to carve out time for the big money stuff. At first, it could be about a third of your time, until you can get the big money projects launched and bringing in coin. Eventually, the pendulum will swing to concentrating solely on the bigger money, biggest love projects. This is where money really does start to equal happiness.

BUT HAVE YOU DONE THE WORK?

We need to distinguish between being "deserving" and actually being "worthy" in order to have this conversation. I'm going to split some spiritual hairs, here: **Every single one of us is deserving.** Fulfillment is our birthright. We deserve love, joy, and comfort. All of it. Inarguably. You deserve what you want. You deserve the best. This is a very spiritual perspective, of course. It presupposes an innate divinity within each and every one of us. It assumes purity and universal oneness.

And this same perspective can be used as a lame excuse for not having to work for what you want. As our society becomes more hooked on immediacy—brighter and whiter in minutes; twenty pounds in twenty days; just Google it; it's, like, taking *forever* for this website to load—we're getting conditioned to think that little effort and quick results are the rule, not the exception. Minimum effort for maximum results is a brilliant productivity goal. But it doesn't translate to doing your homework, being prepared, or growing your value over time. **There's nothing like a sense of entitlement to repel what you want the most.**

Relationships are a great illustrator of how the "but I'm worth it," assumption can get in the way of actually getting what you want. I met Lenny in a tiki lounge. People tend to tell me stuff—stuff they don't tell other people. Even without any vodka involved, this is bound to happen. One drink in and Lenny was baring his soul to me about his heartbreak. "I could never figure out why she wasn't all over me. I'm a total score. Guess it was because I was an asshole." Yep. That's how it works, Lenny. It doesn't matter how great your mama told you you are. Give value. Get valued.

If you're a predominantly self-serving, incessantly demanding partner, are you worthy of adoring attentiveness and getting properly laid on a regular basis? I'm going with . . . *no, not so much*. Do you *deserve* attentiveness and intimacy? Of course you do. You're a child of the universe; you're made of the same stuff as the Seven Wonders of the World. But in real time, your wishes aren't matching up with your actions. Deserving, yes. Worthy, not yet.

VALUE IS A TWO-WAY STREET

In order to attract that which we feel worthy of, we need to believe in our own merits. But we also need to pay attention to what the world is telling us—our customers, our partner, our teammates. Members of our community can sometimes see us more clearly than we see ourselves. If we're really adding value to a situation, people and profits tend to stick around.

The value you have to offer ebbs and flows no matter how evolved or successful you become. One's value can never be a fixed rate. We get better at what we do, we become more conscious and more thoroughly available to the people in our life, we have setbacks, and we have false starts and fresh starts.

In relationships or work or art (all the same thing, really), valuation is a constant dance. It's an interplay of self-knowledge, making requests, giving and taking with the people in your life, and being responded to. Just as gold needs to be mined, molded, and polished to determine its worth, we need to weigh and polish our own value against "what's out there."

Some people have a beautiful sense of self-worth and entitlement—not out of arrogance, but rather in an almost genteel, wise way. They have a core certainty that their needs will be met and that their very presence renders them good enough. *I'm here. I'm good. What have you got for me?*

I always wonder if these types of people had not one but three perfect mothers, and lived a dozen past lives as royalty. Because I, for one, incarnated with the (limiting) belief that I needed to *work it! And work it good!* For the longest time, my value was a "to be determined" proposition—always a moving target. In an effort to earn my keep, my place, and my respect, I was always giving more, more, and even more. I overdelivered to clients and I overcompensated for my partners, both romantic and in business. I did it to be loved, to be profitable, to be deemed truly valuable—and even better, to be thought of as indispensable.

Whatever your paradigm is on deserving, social proof says that one's valuation is, *in part,* set through commerce, through interaction. You can believe with all your heart that you're a smokin' hot *lovah,* or a first-rate manager, or made for greater things, but in reality, that needs to be proven.

Your value delivery can be an exchange of services, goods, ideas, or energy. Whether it's a song, an idea for the team, your master's thesis, or asking a certain someone out for a drink, you won't know the full value of what you're offering until you just put it out there. Do your research. Take some risks. And keep in mind that on your way to the top, you will be required to check your ego here and there. You might even need to peel it off the floor a few times.

Part of determining your value is how determined you are to give value ■

INTEND TO BE WORTH IT

Give it away—*selectively*.

Volunteer two weeks of your time to get the job; offer to take on an aspect of a project without pay; give lots 'n' lots of your goodies away—for free.

I know what you're thinking: "But if I give it away for free, no one will value it. They'll think I'm desperate. They'll take me for granted." I understand. *Selectively* is the operative word here. You don't volunteer for just any organization, and you don't give your stuff away to just anyone who asks for it. The recipients of your love and mad skills need to qualify, darling. You have standards, you have boundaries, and even if you are, in fact, desperate to sell your shizzle or land the job, you have a strategy.

The strategy is this: By selectively giving away your time or goods for free, you are, in effect, creating a laboratory study for yourself to examine the effect you have on the world around you. This is not about charity left to chance. You're beta testing your shizzle.

Let me illustrate: Kelly has a new coaching practice. Kelly needs clients. Kelly offers a "free half-hour coaching session" to anyone who calls. I can guarantee you that *if* anyone actually takes Kelly up on that offer (because, yep, people tend to be leery of free stuff), she will not be attracting the kind of clients who are ready and willing to invest in themselves and her services, and Kelly will end up resenting her freebie clients in a big way.

I'd advise Kelly to create a free "salon meets coaching" in-person event on a hot topic that relates to her expertise. Invite a small group of women, say, friends of friends. Meet in someone's gorgeous living room, a yoga studio, or a great workspace after hours. Perhaps the hot topic is stress and sex. Kelly leads a conversation by asking key questions of the group, and she works her own teaching, fact-finding how-tos, and insights into the experience. Women are taking notes. They're getting inspired and seeing Kelly as a wisdom maven. Now she has five women who will potentially go out and talk up her wisdom and either become clients themselves or refer other people. She also has data—more information and real-life stories about women, stress, and sex that she can write about on her blog or in her new book, or talk about on the local breakfast television show. She could do this same exercise with a group on the phone, or with individuals as one-off events or as an extended program.

Free has a return if you have a plan for making the most of it. Consider "free" the cost of marketing and development. And good karma.

TO GIVE OR NOT TO GIVE?

GUIDELINES FOR DISPENSING YOUR FREE SHIZZLE

Nothing is for free. (Except love.) The giving of free time, products, and services is a form of commerce. What do you want in return for what you're giving? The return for you can be psychological, spiritual, material, or all three. "By giving this away for free I'm building my knowledge, my confidence, my faith." That's a great return on investment. "By giving this away for free, I'm getting feedback, exposure, new prospects, client conversion." Great deal.

When you're clear on your motivations, you'll get better results. If your motivation for giving something away for free has to do with people pleasing and a weighty sense of obligation, hold it. If you're afraid no one will pay for your stuff, stop. If you're feeling coerced or fearful, whatever you give will be soaked with resentment or instability and it won't have the effect you want it to.

Target your ideal customer. Your free shizzle giving may be part of a strategy to identify who your target audience is. And you may, in fact, learn that your market isn't what you thought it was, but those kinds of surprises are rare. If you've done the work of developing a service or product—whether it's bake sale goodies or a sophisticated consultancy—then you should have been creating it all along with the target customer in mind, right? So when you set out on a freebie campaign, be sure to give to the people that you want to be your supporting customers in the long run.

Create an exclusive group to give to. Beta testers, a focus group, happy human guinea pigs: **Set a context for the purpose of the group and you can then manage the group's expectations** for what you're giving them. *This is an experiment. This requires one evening a month for three months. What I ask in return is for you to give me feedback. Please tell your friends. Enter your email in the space provided. . . .*

Act like you're getting paid. This is where penultimate professionalism and class comes in. Just because your customer isn't paying you, doesn't mean you get to slack off. Show up in your Sunday best, give them the best packaging and experience possible, follow up, and express your tremendous gratitude that they're coming to get your goodies.

Set a time limit. Like an intern who works for free only for a semester, your free shizzle dispensation has to have a limited time offer—or you go broke, or crazy.

Take pride in your generosity. Free stuff isn't just an experiment or PR stunt; it is a means of love, and you never know what good will come of it.

When you selectively give away your stuff, you're gaining experience and gathering momentum—you're increasing your value.

YOUR MONEY SHOES NEED TO FIT *JUUUST* RIGHT

My friend Violet was running a nonprofit in New York City. She was new to the game but was doing a bang-up job. She was comfortably satisfied with her starting salary. Then an old cowboy road into town with lots of experience and high expectations for his salary. They gave him his asking price and hired him. On the org chart, he sat below Violet. She was his boss, making 35 percent less than he was.

"It was obvious. If they could find the money to pay Cowboy, whom I was directing—and whom I adored, by the way—they were ethically obligated to pay me more." And they did. Vi got a whopping raise the day Cowboy got his desk. "But it never felt right. It felt inflated and inappropriate. Not that I thought I wasn't doing a great job; I was. But it messed with my head a bit. It just added to the impostor complex I was already nursing. I can't believe I'm saying this, but I would rather have earned it in a more direct way, at least by my own demands, not by getting lucky off of someone else's demands." Violet had a case of ill-fitting money shoes. They can blister.

I learned about money shoes from my super-solid successful business friend Sam. I emailed her late one night for some pronto advice. You know the kind of email. You're wishing you had had the good sense and less silly pride to have asked for advice a week ago, and now you're down to the wire and feeling three shades of flummoxed. *Sammy, Gotta submit this proposal asap . . . um, are you still awake? xoxo* Phone rings. It's Sam. Of course. "Lay it on me, cookie." I lay it on her. She tells me her story. I start taking notes, instantly melting with appreciation.

"When I first started doing big accounts like this, they were a lot more than I'd ever made before," Sam started off. "I knew that my corporate clients had gargantuan budgets, and while the project price tag was huge to me, it wasn't so big to them. My first job was actually worth $100,000, but that was about $70,000 more than I'd ever made before on a project! A massive leap, even though I knew the value of my work and that I was 100 percent capable. Yet I just wasn't comfortable walking around in $100,000 shoes yet. It wasn't about how much I could 'get out of them'; it was about what felt right for me." Sam's like that. Integrity *galore*. Which is why Sam is so widely *adored*.

I pictured my own new money shoes. (Brown leather Prada platforms with gold studs and rivets, if you want to know.) Sam went on. "I knew that in my early days, I was leaving money sitting on the table. But it was more important to feel at ease. You need to be comfortable in your money shoes, or things just won't go right. At some point, you'll start to wobble."

I didn't want to wobble with doubt or value issues. I just wanted to land the gig, do a fantastic job, and leverage that to get the next gig. The thought of going for the maximum budget for the sake of it didn't feel good at all. It felt gamy.

We both agreed that conceivably, I could cost the project out at close to $200,000. But what I felt comfortable with—solid, aligned, very pleased—was $120,000. Cushy. *Juuust* right. I could ratchet up if and when I took on another similar project. I felt honorable, I felt blessed, and I felt like my goal was within reach. And I didn't feel ridiculous pressure to excel and compete. I won that contract and it was one of the most hassle-free, *time-efficient* projects I ever worked on. My profit per hour was outstanding.

When your money shoes fit, you're more agile . . . and sensational.

IT COSTS WHAT IT COSTS

Ruby cooked up a plan to get paid to travel. "I convinced my boss that a cross-country road trip with me pitching our product would be great PR. We'd wrap our logo all over a van, I'd create an event in each city, and I'd splash photos all over Facebook. I'd get to fulfill my wanderlust, and the company would get great exposure with its audience. He was all over the idea."

Ruby was ready to hit the road, all expenses paid. "But then I had to draw up the budget proposal and I started to doubt myself. Leasing the car, gas, lodging expenses, some admin support. I certainly wasn't going first-class but the total cost looked scary to me on paper, and I feared that they'd reject my proposal when they saw the numbers. So I started to whittle and scrimp. I thought, *I can lease a compact car instead of a van. I can crash at friends' places instead of hotels. We can do this in eight months instead of twelve.* It all started to feel dismal.

"My mother talked some sense into me. 'It costs what it costs and that's that,' she told me. Yep, she's a practical one. So I submitted my comfortable-but-not-luxurious budget request and then bit my nails waiting for them to tell me I was way out of line and that I was such a prima donna the whole project was off. Or worse, they found someone who'd do it cheaper—like maybe a desperate intern who'd sleep in hostels and then come back and steal my job." Sometimes you work up a sweat when you take a leap.

"Boss man ran into me in the hallway a few days later. 'Do you want to start the road tour on the West or East Coast?' he asked me. 'West,' I answered, thinking that he was still, you know, collecting information to make his decision. 'Good, good, sounds good,' and he started to head into his office."

"So had he seen the budget yet or what?" I asked Ruby.

"Well, I followed him down the hall—feeling like a fat little puppy, I might add—to ask him just that. And he said, get this, 'It costs what it costs.' All that fretting for nothing. What a dork. Lesson learned! It costs what it costs. And that's *that*!" Yo Mama!

Investigate what the people around you value. Start asking friends about how they got their raises, raised money, raised their prices, or raised their standards. Nine times out of ten, there is a leap involved. Leaps include doubt, faith, and—most often—*satisfaction*.

Before you sell yourself short, read this out loud. Twice:

You don't know until you ask.

More often than not, you get what you ask for.

Professionals have been around the block and they know what it costs.

Going back to ask for more money after the fact will feel next to impossible. Start higher and you can flex for less if need be.

No budget is ever written in stone. If people can see the value, they'll find a way to find the money.

And . . .

Exceptional people get exceptions ■

RECIPROCITY IS A BEAUTIFUL THING

REC-I-PROC-I-TY *(NOUN)*

1. given or felt by each toward the other; mutual: reciprocal respect
2. mutual or cooperative interchange of favors or privileges
3. benefit, consideration, earnings, honorarium, payment, payoff, premium, profit, reward, satisfaction

Selfless giving is a transformative force. And so is healthy opportunism.

Consider the value of what you create for others. An organized social calendar for your family. Peace of mind or direction for clients and coworkers. A profitable business that benefits many. A lovely home vibe. Sage advice. Punctuality. Tenderness and laughter.

Where do you need reciprocity to come from? Your friends, family, boss, customers . . . or . . . yourself?

What form of reciprocity would you like to receive? Greater revenue, public recognition, constructive feedback, a hug when you come home? Or perhaps some quiet time, a love note, or a simple but sincerely spoken "Thank you for taking care of us" is what you need to feel seen, heard, and appreciated.

Even if you give freely, sometimes it's okay to ask for reciprocity. More progress happens on a two-way street.

WHAT'S IT WORTH TO YOU?

I find it quite curious and distressing that the wage gap—the disparity between what men and women make—captures so much attention, when the far more insidious problem is our own proclivity to settle for less.

The real reason underearners are in denial is that they are afraid. An admission of truth makes us accountable to change. Denial keeps us stuck. Recognition sets us free.

—Barbara Stanny, *Secrets of Six-Figure Women*

We need to talk more about money. We need to hear one another's lessons and know-how, blunders and recoveries. We need to start acting like the experts of our own financial destiny and sharing with one another what works and doesn't work in our relationships with money.

I'm fascinated (okay, borderline obsessed) with how much stuff costs, how people make their money, what people put value on. The more money stories I hear, the more I learn about human nature, and the more inspired I get to create a reality that works for me—one in which I determine the value of my time and money, not the stock market or Suze Orman. (Don't get me wrong, I love me some Suze.)

Each of us determines the value of our time and money with every choice we make.

My pie-baking grandma Alma grew up in the Depression. When I visited her, sometimes we'd make "a trip to the bank," which was really a trip to three banks. "Why do you have so many banks, Grandma?"

Her answer, in a hushed voice: "In case one gets robbed." In my seven-year-old mind, I pictured two dudes with sideburns driving up to the bank in their Datsun to make a hit. Alma did wonders with Spam, clipped coupons, and safety-pinned her change purse to her bra. She took maybe three vacations in her entire life and watched an old snowy television because the fancy ones were too "dear." She was neither a lender nor a borrower—even when her family was in need. When she passed on, Alma had, *surprise!* hundreds of thousands of dollars in those bank accounts. That's how she valued her money and how she valued her lifestyle.

Some people will drive a mile out of their way to save a buck. Some of us have it delivered. The "value of a dollar" depends on the spender.

I tend to think of money in the same way I regard time: It's a form of energy. It comes and goes according to my intentions. The clearer my intentions, the more the money flows. Before I decide if I'm going to spend my coin on something, I weigh out the potential for results and pleasure. "Pleasure" has a great range. Sometimes delight is the measurable, other times we're aiming for circuit-blowing ecstasy. And as we all know, in terms of commerce, circuit-blowing ecstasy can be achieved with something as indulgent as a piece of chocolate ganache or as luxy as private race-car driving lessons or as noble as making a donation to your favorite cause.

Before you reach for your wallet or click on "Buy," ask your-self, *Is this going to make me feel fantastic in a way that it actually improves my well-being?* If it's about improving your well-being, that helps rule out impulse and stupid big-ego purchases that are mostly about looking cool. *Is this going to help me get the results that I'm aiming for?* When you're focused on creating an amazing future, you tend to **value the present more.** *Is this going to help other people* (including the people you're purchasing from)? *Is this going to make things easier for me, and free me up so that I can pursue more . . . pleasure?* If the pleasure potential matches your budget, then you've got full clearance to proceed.

First, I consider if something will energize me, and second, I consider the actual dollar cost. This means I can act like a wannabe baroness or a total cheapskate in the span of a minute. Like I did one afternoon in Vancouver International Airport.

I had missed my flight cutoff time by five minutes. For years I'd been dreaming of having an experience at a certain spa in New Mexico. My spa package was booked, and if I didn't arrive that day, my whole fantasy was going to be blown away like a tumbleweed in the Sangre de Cristo Mountains.

I did some quick emotional math. I could book a new flight, toss the old one, charter from another hub. What was this experience worth to me? How much more was I willing to pay to prevent dream devastation? I decided I'd go as high as two thousand bucks to rescue my plans—totally frivolous, and not something I'd ever tell my mother. I resolved to do whatever it took to get there, rationalizing that the euphoria of my mountain healing time would make me more productive and, therefore, I'd make that money back in a snap.

Luckily, I had to pay only a $150 rebooking fee. I was elated that my fantasy holiday was about to come true, and I felt like I was $2,000 ahead in the game. It felt sexy knowing that I was willing to go sugar mama on myself. *Damn, girl, you treat yourself fine.* I picked up my boarding pass, walked to the snack shop, and put some glazed almonds on the counter. "That'll be fifteen dollars."

"For these?" I asked.

"Uh-huh."

"You're kidding. I'm not paying fifteen dollars for a bag of almonds." Fantasies fulfilled: Worth it. Getting ripped off: Not going to happen.

We'll dig into what you truly value in the next worksheet: "Freely Associating with Money."

Raising money? Don't do it until you have to. And then question if you really need to. And then think twice about it. And then get a second opinion.

The boys from *Rework* (Jason Fried and David Heinemeier Hansson) sum up my sentiments on raising money perfectly. Allow me to paraphrase:

> You give up control.
> "Cashing out" begins to trump building a quality business.
> Spending other people's money is addictive.
> It's usually a bad deal.
> Customers move down the totem pole.
> Raising money is incredibly distracting.

When raising money is the right thing to do, get mentors, start sending your banker season tickets, prepare to be out of the office at least 30 percent of the time. Take your vitamins.

All the best things I did at Apple came from (a) not having any money, and (b) not having done it before, ever.

—Steve Wozniak, cofounder of Apple

HOW MONEY FEELS

THERE'S ONLY ONE TIME THAT DOING IT FOR THE MONEY WORKS. . . .

And that's when you have a light at the end of the tunnel and an un-wavering commitment to yourself to transition into doing work that makes you happier, or selling something that you're 100 percent proud of. At any given time you could be juggling a "soul job" and a "ho job." Soul jobs are a full-meal deal: stimulation, inspiration, and cash, all in one. Ho jobs are low on the spiritual fulfillment but can go a long way in financing your art.

If you need to suck it up and take a gig to pay the rent, just do it and spare yourself the "artistic integrity and compromise" judg-ment. Paying the rent is a good thing. Being hounded by credit card collectors is a bad thing. When you suck it up for your own greater good and keep your personal vision front and center, you'll have the stamina to do what needs to be done on all fronts—and depending on how soon you want to stand your dream up, "what needs to be done" is a *lot*. The "Soul + Ho" combo is a double-time gig. And the return can be truly great.

HOW DO YOU FEEL ABOUT DEBT?

Some people can't bear to carry a balance on their MasterCard. Others can be comfortable with tens of thousands of dollars in debt in order to finance their vision. Debt is neither good nor bad—it's how you feel about it that matters.

WHAT'S THE WORST THAT COULD HAPPEN?

Having a worst-case scenario liberates you. Imagining the worst possible thing that could happen if you bomb puts the psyche monsters in their place. The vast majority of us have enough smarts, infrastructure, mental health, and love in our lives that we won't be living out of our cars. You can always waitress, move back in with your folks, borrow money from your brother, go back to your boss, pay it off, and pay it forward. It'd kill ya, but it ain't *really* gonna kill ya. When you get down with the dark possibilities, everything else seems up from there.

MY FAVORITE MONEY ADVICE

Don't spend it before you have it.

—Melody Biringer, self-proclaimed start-up junkie
and founder of more than twenty businesses,
most currently the CRAVE Company

This is such a difficult path when the money finally starts coming in, or you get some serious interest from your biggie client on your biggie proposal, or you finally convince the loan officer at the bank that you're a worthy human being. Hard fact: Before you earn it, you don't have it. Projections and ideals do not equal money in the bank.

Don't spend it when you get it.

—Robert Kent, photographer and philanthropist

My last business partner and I were expecting a mid–six-figure deal for a creative project. Dreams were ballooning. Family was swooning. Our ship was coming in. The deal wasn't even sealed and we had picked out new custom-made sofas.

"That wave of money is going to come in," Rob said over souvlaki, "and it's going to take you right out with it." My dreams of a Dwell prefab house started to crumble. "Listen," Rob continued. "You need to feel the power of sitting on it, of letting it actually feed your creativity. If you spend it when you get it, you'll have to catch up with it, and that will sap your energy."

We didn't listen. We sank most of our deal money into needless company growth. We didn't need to expand. We needed to stay lean and focused. Not long after, we were developing bigger projects to keep up with ourselves. We should have listened to the next piece of advice.

Grow organically.

—Rikia Saddy, marketing strategist

Rikia declined to invest in one of my companies because she thought it was the kind of business that should "grow organically . . . one step leading to the next. Your work needs to build on itself." Those words would echo in my mind when my joint venture all fell apart. And when I started my biggest solo enterprise ever with a core strategy: Go organic.

Follow the money.

—plenty of people

Old business guys love to throw out this adage. It's so true. If you can find out who's making the most money and how, you will solve multiple mysteries of motivation.

FREELY ASSOCIATING WITH MONEY

W O R K S H E E T

QUICK HABIT ANALYSIS

What do you love spending money on?

What do you wildly resent paying for?

What do you consider luxurious?

When, where, and how are you cheap?

When, where, and how are you generous?

RAISE YOUR FANTASY FREQUENCY

What's your most common money *fantasy*? Do you see yourself winning the lottery, getting a big raise, marrying into money, having a top seller, watching your stocks go through the roof, getting a new car at factory prices? If your number one fantasy didn't come true, then what would be your next-best fantasy? If that didn't come through, then what would be ideal? And if *that* didn't happen, then what would be a great way to have money come into your life? And so on.

The point of this exercise is to **imagine as many different ways as possible that money can enter into your life.** Awaken part of your money memories that might be dormant, and consider that money is *everywhere*.

continues on next page

GET EMOTIONAL ABOUT MONEY

STEP 1

Answer the following questions as honestly as you can.
How do you feel:

> About your debt?
>
> About your income?
>
> About your savings and assets?
>
> About anyone who owes you money?
>
> When you pay for experiences and outings?
>
> When you go grocery shopping?
>
> When you shop for gifts?
>
> When you shop for clothes?
>
> When you shop for decor, art, or collectibles?

STEP 2

Identify what pure positivity with money would feel like.

If you have negative feelings that showed up in some of the above answers, think of the positive feelings that counter those. For example, if how you feel about your debt is heavy, burdened, or resentful, perhaps the positive contrast would be promising, empowered, and grateful.

STEP 3

Choose just **one positive money emotion**—the one that feels the most vital and exciting to you—and think of **one action** you can take in **each of the money areas** below that will help you feel that way:

How you spend money

How you save money

How you give money

How you receive money

How you manage money

For example, if the feeling you want the most around money is gratitude, what can you do when spending your money to feel grateful? Is it keeping a gratitude journal for the things you buy, or being extrapolite to sales clerks, or saying a quiet "thanks for the ability to pay my bills" when you're writing a check to the electric company? Say your most positive feeling is security. What can you do in regard to how you manage your money to feel that way? Create monthly cash flow projections, join an investment group, write your will, start a new savings account? There are unlimited ways to create the positive feelings you want in every interaction you have with money.

comrades

cheerleaders

soul sisters bros

united team tribe

collaborating

community

SESSION 14

supporting

characters

In everyone's life, at some time, our inner fire goes out.
It is then burst into flame by an encounter with another
human being. We should all be thankful for those people
who rekindle the inner spirit.

—Albert Schweitzer

There is no union except in the same high effort.

—Antoine de Saint-Exupéry

COLLABORATIVE PARADIGMS

I used to believe that in order to be a solid businesswoman and compassionate human being, I needed to work with people who saw the world in very different ways than I did. I needed to be more tolerant, more open-minded, more flexible. I needed to *diversify*. Oh, how wrong I was. Inevitably, my faux tolerance led to heartache or legal fees.

My friend Steve directed one of the most successful and profitable game development teams in the world, so he knows a lot about getting people to push their creative limits. His theory was that in order to do visionary stuff, you need to create a "culture of yes." A culture of yes isn't about stacking the crew with "yes men" who tell you what you want to hear. It's about surrounding yourself with people who say yes to possibility—people who can appreciate and be motivated by creative insanity. Why would you want to have to convince your collaborators of anything? You shouldn't have to waste energy on converting people to your vision of a great workplace or a life of adventure. Either they believe in the beauty and audacity of your vision, or they don't. Either they're willing to find the way, or they're not. The rest is just navigational coordinates.

Take stock: **Who's on your bus—who are you cocreating with? And how do they see the world?**

Now let's turn that around to get to the power place: How do *you* see the world? This could be a complicated exercise, but pretend it's simple. Are you a glass-half-full or half-empty person? Are you on this side of trusting or that side of cautious? Do you need to see it to believe it, or believe it to see it? In the most sweeping, general terms, how do you regard the human race?

Your worldview is precious stuff. And it should guide the guest list of who you invite on your bus.

Whom do you really *want* to cocreate with? Be idealistic here. Time is precious—why spend it with the kind of people who make you crazy? What do they stand for? What do they value?

You may not always get to choose who you work with or who moves in next door. But when you have a say in whom you get to collaborate or team with, go for people who have shared values and you'll be starting off on solid ground.

I once worked with a "service provider" who believed that trust was something that needed to be earned—that no one could be trusted until they had proved themselves to be trustworthy. She believed that nondisclosure agreements were a general course of order, and that ideas needed to be guarded and dispensed only in increments. Her primary negotiation tool was to withhold information and emotion. Lots of people operate this way. Some businesses necessitate it. Paranoia insists on it. I'd feel more satisfied digging ditches.

After my faux flexibility led to strife and shallow threats, I finally had to fess up to the fact that I actually prefer to hang with . . . *happy* people. Trusting people. And damn it, I *like* idealists. I finessed my criteria for friends and teammates: If you want to get on my bus you've got to believe that a trusting heart is a strong heart, because trust is a form of love and stamina.

Secondly, you've got to operate on the premise that everything happens for a reason. That even setbacks are progress. That there is some divine sensibility to how all of this is unfolding—that there is some order to this chaos. You can be cynical. You can rock like Spock, but you won't be getting a VIP pass to my party unless you've got some cosmic faith. And that's what I call having standards.

Once we get those fundamentals checked off, *then* it's time to diversify. I don't care if you're a right-wing Baptist, a Buddhist, a crystal-polishing New Ager, or a devout or recovered Catholic—we've got enough yes-ness to make some major progress together.

Once you've created a baseline for entry then you can mix and contrast skills and ambitions with one another's strengths and weaknesses. And that's when the party really starts.

YOU DESERVE YOUR TRIBE

Each of us is here for a brief sojourn; for what purpose he knows not, though he sometimes thinks he senses it. But without deeper reflection one knows from daily life that one exists for other people.

—Albert Einstein

As Seth Godin defines it, "a tribe is any group of people, large or small, who are connected to one another, a leader, and an idea . . . you can't have a tribe without a leader—and you can't be a leader without a tribe."

You may be the leader of the productive, eco-friendly guys in their thirties with kids tribe; or the tribe of beauty and old-fashioned manners; or yoga and self-expression; glamorous self-love; satisfaction for singles; fashion that cares; art that heals; business with heart; or punk rock illumination. It doesn't matter what the ilk or industry is, if you're leading others to what you love and believe, you've gone tribal.

When you hang with your tribe, you feel invigorated, recognized, and understood—you can't underestimate the powerful effects of being fortified in that way. When you have your tribe on speed dial, you've got all the resources you need to fuel up, fly straight, and head back out to face the world at large.

ADVISORY BOARDS, OBJECTIVITY + RAH-RAH

Meetings with your advisory board can be formal and regulated, or they can be breakfast a few times a year with a seasoned millionaire who'll tell you why you'd better fish or cut bait before your money dries up. Maybe it's a glass of wine on a Thursday night with a friend who calls it straight, with love.

My own advisers have taken many forms over the years: a former professional skier who knew a lot about teamwork, a business coach who challenged me to loosen my grip on my so-called identity, a Buddhist psychotherapist, and a girlfriend who had both an MBA and a bachelor of social work (which is a wicked combination of greatness). I've called on magazine editors for pitch advice, venture

Create your support system before crisis comes ■

capitalists for partnership counsel, a political consultant for branding strategies, a psychic naturopath for get-me-to-my-deadline
supplements, and astrologers for best-days-to-launch insight. It
takes a village.

It's good to have advisers lined up before you urgently need
them. So often we think, *Oh, I'm doing fine, growing right along,*
and maybe you are, until you're not anymore—until the market or
karma throws you a curveball.

Don't be afraid to make the cold call: "Hi. I'm a fan of your work
and I'd like to have tea and here's precisely why. . . . I'm not a crazy
stalker. I'm actually pretty accomplished and insightful . . . and I
respect your time . . . and your wisdom. How's next week look for
you?" Rally the girls: "My place, tonight. I'll order in. Gotta solve
this by Friday." And if what you're up to requires fancy advisory
meetings with voting procedures, serve *paniers chocolats* or some
Red Bull. Formalities need celebration. Some support relationships
will fizzle over time, and you'll get sour advice once or twice, but
your cosmic crew will be what keeps you out of the psych ward in
the long run.

CONSCIOUS WORK PARTNERSHIPS

I'm not going to delve too deeply into the dynamics of romantic love
(I'm still figuring that out for myself), but I do want to talk about
business partnerships for a minute.

You've signed the lease; you're high on possibility; you love that
your strengths and weaknesses "complement each other." You're in
it to win it. What could go wrong?

Everything.

If my betrothed asked me to sign a prenup, I'd probably walk
the other way. But when it comes to the business of making art or

money, you gotta *hollah* for a prenup, sugar. Get your terms of understanding in writing. Here's why, just for starters:

The mere exercise of developing a partnership agreement will illuminate the unspoken fears and foibles that usually stay hidden until things get fractured. The process will also bring forth the beautiful synergies and intentions that make the union so potentially rewarding.

When you invest in the process, you affect the outcome. There are the nuts and bolts of an agreement—percentages, shares, the numbers, and the legal rights. Carving out those material matters will likely bring up some emotion—and it's better to have it brought to the surface than pushed aside. You're laying the groundwork here for how you will continue to make important decisions, manage change, and respond to tough times together.

But I'm also talking about working through the *essence* of your partnership—the very spirit of the relationship. Chemistry, dynamic, purpose. This is what drives the partnership in such a critical way. Who's in charge of what; how will you deal with conflict, tragedy, setbacks, and success? What's brought you together? What's the attraction or the necessity? **Why are you relying on each other, and what are you relying on each other for?**

If you can't face your present-day fears directly, then you're ill-prepared for harsh realities. And that's the prickly, uncomfortable work that needs to be done when cocreating agreements. You need to take into account your concerns as they relate to your partner's history. "Historically speaking, you don't complete things. If you don't finish projects, how are we going to handle that?" It's not an easy conversation to have. And then come tragic possibilities. "If you get hit by a bus and your company shares transfer to your spouse, there's no way that they can take a role in the company." If you can make it through the agreement-building process, you clear the runway to really soar.

EXPERT HELP = QUANTUM LEAPS

I heart experts. Masters. Focused generalists. Theology professors, astrologers, nutritionists, dog-behavior specialists, ordained lamas, makeup artists, code-commanding geeks, landscape designers. Deeply knowledgeable and widely informed people who know their very particular stuff.

Expertise can be expensive. If we are strapped for cash and overworked, it's completely understandable that so many of us hunker down and try to do it all ourselves. But the right advice could save you, make you thousands of dollars, or cut months off your learning curve. Sometimes you pay big bucks for it (it's usually worth it), but oftentimes there are ways to get that kind of expertise for free—sometimes it's as simple as asking.

THEY'RE RIGHT: DON'T BURN BRIDGES

My onetime boss John gave me this counsel, and at the time I thought this was a staid and stodgy convention. Yawn—I'd heard it a hundred times. And how could I possibly stomach being nice to so-and-so? I was outta there and not looking back. But John went on to philosophize, and it got through to me. "The world is a small town, and you never know when you're going to circle back and need someone. Besides, it's rarely worth telling someone off. There's always something better to do with your time."

On the whole, bridge preservation is simply about extending basic kindness and dignity to all parties. And that's always a good thing.

SIZING UP SIMPATICO

WORKSHEET

PAR-A-DIGM *(NOUN)*

a set of assumptions, concepts, values, and practices
that constitutes a way of viewing reality

YOUR WORLDVIEW.
IN SHORT.

Here's what we're going for: **a pithy summation of your life philosophy.** Write a short poem that says it all. Say it in iambic pentameter, in 140 characters or less, or fashion it as a campaign statement. Shake out the most meaningful words with these questions and then hone your declaration.

I think that most people are:

I believe that life is:

I hold the opinion that:

I'm the kind of person who:

I relate to people who are:

I love people who:

People who think that _____ make me _____.

My evil twin would be very:

I have faith that:

I see my work as a means to:

What I value most in myself is:

What I value most in other people is:

I cherish working with people who:

SUPPORT TEAM INVENTORY

WORKSHEET

Which of these four experts could help you take your life to the next level? Which experts would you have to pay for? Which ones could you take a class from, read the work of, watch the videos of, or ask out for coffee? Which expert types are already in your life in the form of friends, colleagues, family? How can you formalize those expert exchanges? Who will you make strides to connect with?

MOTIVATION + STRATEGY

Business coach

Life coach

Partnership coach

Money coach

Voice coach

Therapist

Spiritual adviser

Mentor

WELLNESS + IMAGE

Healer/doctor

Intuitive

Nutritionist

Astrologer

Naturopath

Massage therapist

Personal trainer

Fitness instructor

Child care provider

Interior decorator

Stylist (clothing)

Hairstylist

Personal shopper

SYSTEMS
+ CREATIVE

Financial planner

Investment adviser

Accountant

Bookkeeper

Graphic designer

Web designer

Search engine
   optimization adviser

Lawyer

Trademark agent

Virtual assistant

Personal organizer

Marketing strategist

Branding strategist

Copywriter

Ghostwriter

Editor

Handyman

House boy/chick who feeds
   you grapes while you're
   checking your email

REPRESENTATION

Talent agent

Literary agent

Speaking agent

Publicist

Publisher

generously

giving useful charity

optimism

helping hands lifting

love

SESSION 15

be the giver

This is the true joy in life, the being used for a purpose recognized by yourself as a mighty one; the being thoroughly worn out before you are thrown on the scrap heap; the being a force of Nature instead of a feverish selfish little clod of ailments and grievances complaining that the world will not devote itself to making you happy.

—George Bernard Shaw, poet

Of all the fires, love is the only inexhaustible one.

—Pablo Neruda, poet

You're here. You showed up. That would indicate that there's probably more love, intelligence, and coin where that came from. Your heart may be broken, you may not have enough money to get to the end of the week, you may be fighting for your life. But by many accounts, even in tough times, most of us are remarkably fortunate. By many accounts, **you and I have every conceivable advantage to being happy, healthy, and deeply fulfilled.**

Make generosity part of your growth strategy. Don't wait. Don't wait until your stuff is selling or you've got enough of a cushion in your bank account. Don't wait until you've got more time. Give now.

If you're breathing, you have something to give ▪

Just be the Giver. Please. Be the generous one, the mentor, the adviser, the motivator, the donor, the donator, the one who cares. Find a way to make what you do matter for more people, or matter more for one person. Give someone a break. Give someone hope. Make a promise. Keep it. Overdeliver. Open the door of opportunity; open your wallet. Open your heart, take out the love, and hand it to someone.

DON'T HOLD BACK

That I spent, that I had; that I gave, that I have;
that I left, that I lost.

—Robert Byrkes, A.D. 1579

There are three reasons we resist giving: We feel separate from ourselves, we feel separate from others, or we feel separate from life itself. This sense of disconnection fosters the illusion that either we have less to give, or that we need to get more for ourselves. Depleted or Entitled = Separate.

If we see ourselves mistreated by and separate from those around us, we might orient to what we can get from the external world—who owes us, how we can give ourselves an advantage, how we can game the system. We focus on who's done us wrong, all the things we never got from our parents, the privileges that our cousins had but we didn't, and how easy it was for a buddy to get the job that we wanted. This brand of bitterness is fertile ground for cynicism and *me versus them* thinking, and this notion, which is deadly in terms of generosity: *I worked for what I have, and you should, too.*

Or, perhaps, in our feelings of deficiency we may not think we're even worthy of getting more for ourselves. We take what we get and we make do with it. We don't see how we could possibly add value to the conversation or our communities. This, of course, is the most tragic falsity that is borne of feeling cheated or unloved.

There is the fog of ignorance that stalls us from giving. We grow up sheltered—whether we're rich kids or project housing kids, toughened or contented. Due to various circumstances, we simply don't know life beyond our own reality. Some of us will live and die in the safe bubble of our own culture. You can't force empathy, but you can always access sympathy—it lives in your heart. Hopefully life leads us to a new doorway and we not only witness varying states of democracy, suffering, and ingenuity on the planet, but we're also moved enough to contribute to a cause greater than our own life maintenance—and then eventually, maybe, giving will become a given.

GET CLOSER TO THE PAIN

Give until it hurts.

—The Dalai Lama

Giving can break your heart in half. It's logical to protect yourself.

Once upon a time, I was a Perfume Girl. You know, one of those babes who stand in the cosmetics aisle of department stores asking if you'd like a spritz of the latest sniffy *le fou fou*? That was me. In heels and shoulder pads.

Every day on my way to work, I'd see the same street busker outside the turnstile door playing for coins. He was absolutely gorgeous. Tall and dark, with soft brown eyes. Think Hugh Jackman with a French accent. He was *oo la la* Parisian. Always smiling. He played the accordion in a white blouse and sneakers and sang Édith Piaf. And he also wore . . . a clown nose.

The dignity. The humility. It broke my heart.

I couldn't take my eyes off him, but I could hardly look at him. And so I never tossed him so much as a nickel. All those days. Five days a week. I just watched the tourists and little kids walk up and drop money in his purple velvet-lined accordion case.

I wondered how his life had come to this—singing for change in front of the Hudson's Bay Company department store. And I then read about him in the community newspaper. His name was Marc. "I hope to be able to make nice Christmas for my family." (Not-so-perfect English.) He had a family. He really needed those tossed coins.

Before each payday I was usually down to my last ten bucks, just enough for bus fare to work and a burrito. One day I mustered up my confidence and clip-clopped over to his accordion case. In a silly flurry I dropped in a fiver and kept walking. I then made a sharp turn into the nearest alley, buried my face in my purse, and sobbed.

I felt complicit in his humiliation. I felt ashamed of how many times I'd walked by without looking him in the eyes. I felt poor.

But I saw what I needed to see in that flood of shame: **Sometimes we resist giving because it hurts to meet others in their place of need and suffering. Sometimes, it's easier to make ourselves separate than to enter into someone else's sphere of pain.**

Generosity insists that you meet people where they are. This requires some courage, like all forms of intimacy. If we can stop circling the pain, our natural curiosity will pull us closer to it. And when we move toward it, we find the riches of compassion.

GIVE WHAT YOU CAN

Spiritual practice is returning again and again
to softness.

—Stephanie Dowrick, *Seeking the Sacred*

EVEN FAKE SMILES CAN MELT HEARTS

Harville Hendrix is one of the world's most well-known love therapists. His approach in *Getting the Love You Want* can open up new
fields of possibility in a relationship. One of his beliefs is that each
person in a couple should articulate, with great precision, what they
need from the other. While it's understood that we are ultimately
responsible for our own happiness, and that it is not our partner's
duty to fill us up, Hendrix believes that part of love is endeavoring
to meet some of those precise needs of the person you're with.
Basic. Romantic. And, potentially, incredibly annoying.

His advice for doing what your honey needs to feel loved: Fake
it if you need to. Act like you like it. Just give it. And then get ready
for your cranky little heart to melt right open. Say you're all pissy
because your partner's love request is that when he gets home, you
peel your face off the computer screen and actually go to the door
to greet him. "It would really make me feel like I mattered, babe."
It's easy. But you're busy. And it just bugs you. *Of course* he matters. What difference does it make if you dash to the door or saunter
over when you're good and ready?

But you force yourself to give it. You hear the keys in the front
door, you clench your teeth, and heave your form up. You sigh
under your breath. And then you put on your best smile and you

Generous people have more to give ■

give it. And there's your sweetheart with groceries in one arm and you in the other, feeling like he's the only person in the world in that moment. And a little love is made manifest. And you soften up. And it might occur to you, if even subconsciously, that *this givin' thing ain't so bad*. And tomorrow, or maybe the next week, you'll walk more quickly to the door. And you'll be smiling before you get there, for real.

WHAT HAPPENS WHEN YOU GIVE

That's why we're here—
to make a dent in the universe.

—Hugh MacLeod, *Evil Plans*

Givers get given to.

—Russell Simmons, *Super Rich*

Giving is the antidote to emptiness. It is the meaning we seek, the cure for soul wounds, the spark of enlightenment. Generosity is the traction of spiritual evolution: We give, we grow.

Be the giver.

You'll surprise yourself with your capacity for bliss.

You'll make friends. You will smile more.

You'll bend time and heal the past.

You'll feel richer, healthier, shinier.

You'll feel vulnerable and mighty. Tender and indestructible.

When you give it, you cross that sacred divide where love is no longer a concept but is your soul made manifest. You. Alive.

Gorgeous.

philosophies

in action

SESSION 16

Now is blessed
The rest
Remembered

—**Jim Morrison,** *Wilderness*

Ready, aim, fire? Fire. Fire. Fire.

—**Peter Senge,** *The Fifth Discipline*

A CREDO FOR
MAKING IT HAPPEN

1. **"I'll figure it out"** is the mantra of choice. Accordingly, this buzz kill must be stricken from the lexicon: "I just don't know what to do."

2. If you've never done it before, remember that **everything you've ever done or has happened to you in your entire life and the history of humankind has brought you to this point**—that's a whole lot of life force on your side.

3. If you've done it before, **do it like it's the first time.** A beginner's mind is open and an open mind innovates.

4. Respect the fact that **doubt is part of the creative process.** Examine it as soon as it surfaces. Appreciate that it keeps you alert.

5. **Ask yourself what you're going to give up to get where you want to go.** You can't have it all or do it all. But you can always have and do great things.

6. **Aim for passion, not balance.** Balance is a myth. Passion will put your life into the right proportions that work as a whole.

7. **Tell people what you're up to.** When you declare it and share it you're accountable and helpable.

8. **Don't let the desire for perfection become procrastination.** Every novel ever written might have been better. Every piece of technology, every masterpiece, every day—it all might have been even better. So just launch and learn.

9. **Everything is progress.** As any astrophysicist will tell you, the universe is always expanding. That includes you.

10. **Do what you say you're going to do.** This is the single most powerful behavior for success.

11. **Keep it pointed to where you want it to go.** Do a little more of what you really want to be doing every day, and a little less of what you don't want to do, until eventually your reality is brimming with the real ideal.

Your way begins at the other side.
Become the sky.
Take an axe to the prison wall.
Escape.
Walk out like someone suddenly born into color.
Do it now.

    —Rumi

THE "I DON'T KNOW" CONSPIRACY

You're staring up at your ideal life. It's a mountain of treasures piled high in front of you. It's in the near distance, but there are plenty of obstacles on the path between you and getting there. There are problems and some obligations at your feet. You've got to un-tangle some messy preprogramming that's fuzzing up your mind: Your heart aches with the longing to achieve, you need money for the first of the month, you want to quit eating fast food, and your dreams of happiness are making you envious of others.

A new gig, a crumbling relationship, financing, sharper skills, higher connections, a quagmire of doubts, a gorgeous tabula rasa. Wide open space for mad crazy bliss. It's all there. You can barely sit still.

And then this leaks in: *I don't know where to start.*

Or this toxic implosion happens: *I just don't know what to do.*

If you declare you don't know, then you won't . . . know. You'll just sway back 'n' forth in the lull of *duh*. There will be no urgent need to bust a move because really, you just don't want to . . . know how to. Knowing where to start would change things. Knowing what to do would mean that you could take action, immediately. Knowing is edgy. Not knowing is kinda comfy.

If you said to your commanding officer in a training exercise, "I don't know what to do," you'd be scrubbing the latrine in short order. If you said that in combat, you might be dead. If you told your heartbroken significant other that you were willing to make the changes they had begged for but then said, "I just don't know what to do," well, it wouldn't foster much mojo or trust, would it? If the idea fairy dropped a fat opportunity on your desk and you told her, "But I don't know where to start," she wouldn't be too impressed.

LEAD YOUR LIFE

You're stronger, and you're better, and you're ready for whatever.

—Alicia Keys, "Wait Til You See My Smile"

Give assurances. Spiff up your self-talk. Speak properly when you're in the presence of your sacred ambitions. Trick yourself if you need to. "Dunno, but if I *did* know, then here's what I'd do."

Reframe: You're staring up at your ideal life. There are plenty of obstacles on the path between you and your ideal. You might be in a tough spot or painful circumstances. Things might seem bloody impossible. You may be tuckered out.

And then this: "I'll figure it out."

And again, because courage always echoes: "I'll figure it out."

How's that feel? Much better, doesn't it? More . . . possible. More upright. Wings ready to spread. Ears piqued to hear universal cues. Instincts at the helm. You can still be confused and scared. But when you're determined, fear takes a backseat, not the steering wheel.

"I'll figure it out" may mean waiting patiently for the answer to come. It may mean tirelessly turning over every stone. It may mean praying till you sweat, surveying the experts, or forty days in a proverbial desert. But one thing's for sure: **If you declare that you'll figure it out, the possibilities are endless.**

You've never been where you're going. You'll figure it out. You're the only one who can.

CAKE WALKS + FIRE WALKS: BEGINNER'S MIND

In the beginner's mind there are many possibilities,
but in the expert's mind there are few.

—Shunryu Suzuki, Zen master

The ability to start out upon your own impulse is
fundamental to the gift of keeping going upon your
own terms. . . . Getting started, keeping going,
getting started again—in art and in life, it seems
to me this is the essential rhythm.

—Seamus Heaney, poet

I walked on hot coals once. Barefoot. Across a bed of white hot embers about twenty feet long. When you step off the coals and into the little puddle of water that's waiting for you, you can hear your tootsies steaming. And when you hear that *tssssst* sound, and see that not only do you have all ten toes remaining, but not even a blister, you feel pretty freaking . . . *freaked out,* but in a newbie X-Men mutant euphoric kind of way.

I raced home from the fire-walking workshop at midnight, under a full moon, with a note card tucked into my Levis: "I, Danielle LaPorte, walked on fire. I can do anything." (The instructor had us write these cards; I went with it.) The idea was that anytime we felt less than heroic, we could look at that three-by-five index card stuck on our bathroom mirror, and remember that we bent matter with our minds and therefore have access to special people powers. Handy.

Would I do it again? I hesitate. The evening of that fire walk seminar I asked some of the repeat walkers how the night went for them. I was really surprised to hear that some people burned their feet on what was their second or third time walking. The prevailing response: "Yeah, but I got cocky this time around. I didn't approach it with a fresh mind."

Ask any athlete or elite performer, writer, salesperson, speaker, very big project manager, or wide-awake lover: A track record can dull your senses. Each win has got to be a new win, earned with intense focus and an open heart.

Do not take your expertise for granted. Stay awake. Hunt. Kill your old material. Listen for new information. Tell the story in a different way. Kiss like it's your first kiss. Crush your gimmicks. Make no assumptions. Let the page be white. Then and only then, begin.

THE POWER OF BEING POSITIVELY DOUBTFUL

The greater the artist, the greater the doubt.
Perfect confidence is granted to the less
talented as a consolation prize.

— Robert Hughes, art critic

A painter friend of mine once said that having an art show is like "pulling down your pants in public." Someone said that acting "is like being naked on stage and turning around—very, very slowly." Nerves are part of displaying your art, and doubt keeps you modest. You can make performance anxiety work in your favor.

Being smug dulls your senses—and irritates the people around you. If you're not even slightly doubtful or anxious about your performance, talents, contributions, or big presentation, then you better generate yourself some doubt to keep yourself watchful and in the game.

Vulnerability is strength. Composure is *bella,* but coy is a drag. Speak your feelings: *I'm nervous. I really, really want this to work out. I've been anticipating this for so long.* Don't be reluctant to show your excitement. When you step into that vulnerable place, you're stepping into your presence, and from there you access your power. Bring all of you forward, along with your doubts, fears, and hesitations.

BELIEVE IN YOUR BEST INTENTIONS

Sometimes we have to toss a dream up in the air, like releasing a homing pigeon, and trust that it's going to come back to us with some mission-critical information. We can't control the outcomes of our wishes; we can control only the wishing. We have to leave room for surprise, new longings, unplanned diversions, and the odd disaster to happen. All you can be sure of is that you're here to be you and to do some good. That truth will be your North Star.

Sincerity is a winning formula ■

PRACTICALITY + AMBITION

I love crazy ambition. Crazy gets stuff *done*. Crazy eats impossible for her three o'clock sugar fix. But there's a stupid kind of crazy ambition that's best to avoid. **Stupid crazy ambition is the unrealistic, delusional (and often inflated) thought that you can accomplish big, fast, amazing things while keeping the rest of your life in a state of balance.**

It's the superhero syndrome: *I can do it all! I can squeeze more hours out of the day, keep up my exercise regime, be romantically attentive, well groomed 'n' stylin', AND launch a brilliant, innovative, substantive product in record time. Nothing will change. I'll just fit MORE in.*

Of course you have to do *more*. You have to expand in order to reach new heights. But that capacity needs to be poured directly into your project, not spread thin among preexisting obligations and habits. Accomplishing great things quickly isn't a function of a broader focus; it's a function of laser focus.

Ask yourself what you're going to have to give up in order to pull it off. It's a total downer of a question, and superheroes hate this part of strategy. Innovation by nature is disruptive, not accommodating. Something will have to give so the greatness has room to emerge. Give stuff up so it doesn't take you down. **Clear the decks.** Tell your friends they won't hear from you for the next few months. Forgive yourself in advance for missing birthdays and social gatherings. Put your favorite sushi take-out place on speed dial. Cancel your cable TV. Alert anyone and everyone involved in your crazy project that it's tunnel vision time.

Twyla Tharp calls it the creative bubble and believes it's the zone in which she creates her best work. "I eliminated every distraction, sacrificed almost everything that gave me pleasure, placed myself in a single-minded isolation chamber, and structured my life so that everything was not only feeding the work but subordinated to it." Twyla's hard-core. I think you should leave plenty of room for pleasure in every process. But either way, you need to create your version of the creative bubble to help you get the job done.

That kind of radical focus is the practical response to crazy ambition. What's nuts—as in unrealistic and delusional and kind of insane—is thinking that you can do big, fast, amazing professional things while keeping the rest of your life in a pretty-looking state of balance. It doesn't exist. Crazy ebbs. And sanity flows. Part of being practical is knowing just what it takes to make amazing stuff—it takes a lot of fantastic, hard work.

Line up some "multidimensional" support. When it's nose-to-the-grindstone time, we tend to get the grindstone kind of people on board—suppliers, designers, editors, marketers, "work/task" people. But this is precisely the time when you need some spiritually informed intelligence to back you up: a naturopath, a trainer, green smoothies, a prayer group. All that woo-woo love and insight will go a long way in helping you navigate the heavy-duty logistics on a daily basis.

Declare your intentions as widely as possible. Announce that you're going "away" for a while. When you're proactive about announcing your short-term utter neglect and blatant unavailability to the rest of the world, you solve some problems before they start.

Half of getting where you want to go is knowing what it takes to get there. Crazy ambition requires radical practicality. Otherwise, it's just stupid.

THE MYTH OF BALANCE

If consensus is overrated, I think balance is, too.
I have no interest in living a balanced life.
I want a life of adventure.

    —Chris Guillebeau, *The Art of Non-Conformity*

In the end, the quest for balance is bogus.
Love your burdens. Love them hard. And when
your loves knock you down or your weak ankles
trip you up, stop worrying about balancing
—'cuz you're not—and bounce.

    —Kelly Diels

The pursuit of balance is stressing us out. It's a maddening juggle of self, others, career. Equal parts exercise, home décor, loverly devotion, career ambition, and family tending—and we wonder why we get sick when we finally take a vacation.

If you do manage to get balanced, it's only temporary. Success throws things out of whack. Just when you get it balanced, circumstances or a great idea turns everything around. You can never get it right. Balance: the losing battle.

I burn a lot of omelets. It's a regular occurrence. I'm drawing robots with my kid, I'm jotting down an idea I don't want to lose, I'm taking the call. And then the smoke alarms go off. I "work" on holidays. I've been known to read in bed all day on a Monday. I send birthday gifts three months early or three months late, but I always send just the right gift. I can eat granola cereal every day for a week, wear the same clothes, and not leave the house because I want to finish a project. The last time I was at a monastery, I tweeted about it. This is not a balanced life. But it works for me.

Striving for balance will derail your plans for greatness. Do you think that Leonardo da Vinci or Amelia Earhart or Richard Branson set out thinking, "I want to live a balanced life"? No. Their aim was on audacity, full expression, and all the boundaries that they were compelled to break.

THE MUSICALITY OF YOUR LIFE

The antidote to exhaustion isn't rest.
It's wholeheartedness.

—David Whyte, poet

Think of the totality of your life as a symphony. Great music has dimension and layers that compose the overall harmony. It's not about making sure each instrument is played at the same volume all at once—that would be droning. There is a time for the strings to carry it all, and for the drums to take it in a new direction, and for the trumpets to punctuate. There is a time when your relationships matter more than your job. There will be months when your career sets the pace of your entire life. There will be passages when your focus is inward and you retreat from the surface of your life to tend to your body and soul.

Balance doesn't exist, but proportion and harmony do.

Your work. Your relationships. Your inner life. In his book of the same name, David Whyte calls these "the three marriages."

"Each of the three marriages is nonnegotiable. They cannot be 'balanced' against one another—a little taken from this and a little given to that—except at their very peripheries. To 'balance' work with relationship and with the self means we only work harder in each marriage, while actually weakening each of them by separating them from one another." These fundamental components of our existence must work to support one another, not to vie for unfaltering attention.

Sadly, we frequently and unconsciously structure our lives so that our work, our spirit, and our significant relationships are set against one another in a competition of importance. Someone or something is bound to lose in this equation. When we deny one of the fundamentals of our life the attention it's asking us for, our whole life is affected. We ignore our creative calling to keep the peace in our household, and we feel a gnawing resentment that spills into how we treat the very people we are trying to please. We work late, again, when our partner is in genuine and serious need, and the guilt of our neglect stifles both the joy of the partnership and the joy of our work.

To be a whole person we need to fully recognize that we have these very distinct parts of our life, and that each part needs to be honored and tended to. We must consider what our vocational calling is and how we will serve in the world, via jobs or the free offering of our talents and resources. Whether we're a monastic, the revered family matriarch, or a drifter, we must become aware of how we give and receive love. And we must define ourselves outside of the day-to-day and contemplate the divine nature of who we are.

To ignore one of the major aspects of our existence is like refusing to go beyond our own front door—we limit our access to *everything*.

To harmonize our life, we need to let each part of it have center stage when it feels most urgent and ripe. Some of this timing is universally seasonal—leaving home, forging identities as we forge our livelihood, putting down roots, making midlife renovations, and so forth. But ultimately the timing is profoundly personal. You never know when your soul is going to send you a new set of directions via your daydreams or intuition: *Time to uproot. Time to make my art. Time to find my people.*

PASSION IS THE PLOTLINE

It's not the imbalances of life that will get you down—it's doing meaningless things that aren't taking you where you want to go. The more you pursue what you're passionate about at any given time, the less friction and more fluidity you'll have in your life. And that's the definition of harmony.

How does the screw-life-balance-and-go-for-passion theory apply when you're juggling P & Ls and macaroni and cheese? Remember, you're not aiming for perfection and evenly sliced pieces of the life pie. You're creating satisfaction.

It's a work hard / play hard equation. You may drain your reserves because that's what feels satisfying. You'll fill them up again. You may work your ass off and love every minute of it, until one day you cash in and check out. You may abandon your obligations for adventure. It's a wonky equation—creating works of art always is—but if you don't stress about how you "should do it," you can create the best way for you to do it.

When passion is a priority—passion for family, for vocation, for meaning—your energy intensifies. And when your energy is more focused, more "aimed," you begin to care less about the things that don't really matter. You reach out and get the help you need to pull off the important things. You avoid crappy jobs; you stop trying to control the people around you; you complain less and appreciate more.

Full-on living includes fantastic productivity and immense still-ness, self-centeredness and self-sacrifice, time to flare and space to fizzle. Up close, or by the standards of those who prefer the safety of balance, it may look off-kilter, but when you step back, you might see a masterpiece called *Your Life, Lived*. Priceless.

THIS IS IT: THE SECRET TO SUCCESS

Here it is. You heard it here first:

Do what you say you're going to do ■

Don't blow it off, assume that they'll forget what you said, hope that they didn't really hear you, or believe that it's kosher to let it slide. Letting it slide is a slippery slope that leads to sleepless nights and eroded integrity, all of which adds up to one big mess.

Aim for impeccable. There's a great scene in *Jerry Maguire* where one of the Zig Ziglar–like "mentor guys" in a polyester suit says, in his heavy southern accent, "If I do not return yer call within twenty-four hours, well then, you can rest assured that I am dead." He's reliable. I want *that* guy on my team.

Mean it.

"I'll call you tomorrow." . . . "I'll send you the link." . . . "I'll do my best." If you don't mean it with every bone in your body, then just don't say it. Pause. Say thank-you. Say how you feel. Say nothing at all. Habitual convo-filler sucks wind. I can't scientifically prove it, but empty promises are bad for the ozone.

Of course, you can't always do what you said you would. Minds change, and some prerogatives need their exercise. Batteries die, tragedies happen, the best of intentions get rained out. When you can't or choose not to honor your word, then just say so. Tell the truth, tell it fast, and deliver it with sincerity and care. Words are arrows. Take aim.

Enough of these phrases, conceit and metaphors,
I want burning, burning, burning.

—Rumi

WHAT'S IT GOING TO TAKE?

We usually use that phrase in urgent circumstances: What's it going to take?

What's it going to take for you to wake up? What's it going to take for me to quit? What's it going to take for them to realize?

But life is an urgent circumstance, really, when you think about it. Birth: miraculous. Survival: amazing. Death: inevitable. Suffering: optional. Life: urgent.

What would our days be like if we approached happiness with the urgency and insistence that we give to deadlines and should-dos? We've *got* to meet our dancing quota! Come hell or high water, I will stroll in the park today! Wild horses couldn't keep me from lunch with my friends! Top priorities: to meander, to laugh, to look people in the eye.

So, in the spirit of urgent vitality, and not knowing when death may call, and being acutely bored of the same old pattern of complaints, I'm asking myself, and you, lovingly, emphatically:

What's it going to take for us to surface the luminosity and joy that is our true nature? What's it going to take for us to make evolutionary leaps as artists, lovers, friends, citizens, innovators? What's it going to take to get us to prioritize the sacred, to be the first one to say the kindest thing possible, to liberate and optimize our truth?

The answer is incredible:
It will take all of us, being all of who we are.
Light the way.

FUTURE GRATITUDE

WORKSHEET

You are in the perfect position to get there from here.

—Abraham-Hicks

Next month, next year, or five to twenty years down the road, what or who will you be valuing? Why will you be filled with appreciation?

Be practical or big *dream-a-delic*. For example: "It's one year from today and I am so grateful that I own this new home with great light. It's my birthday and I am rocking out in Buenos Aires. Next week, I'm going to be totally thankful that my dad and I had that talk. My health is excellent and the love of my life is by my side. It's 2020 and my phone is ringing off the hook after winning the Nobel Peace Prize (finally!)."

What will you be immensely grateful for?

GREAT, FULL

I forged you with my speech,
No longer bereft, you blaze.

—Emily Warn, poet

How each of the following people propelled me, inspired me, saved my ass, and set me straight is the stuff of legend.

My exclusive Fire Starter clients: I feel privileged to have heard so many dreams and ideas. Being entrusted with your visions has been one of the most nourishing experiences. Deep bow.

In 2009, I took my show on the road and hit sixteen cities with **my Fire Starter groups.** People opened their homes to me and to the lovely strangers who showed up. From Dallas to New York, I experienced great kindness, vibrant people wanting to do good things in the world, and plenty of questions that sharpened my mind and softened my heart. For everyone who hosted and attended, thank you so very much.

At the end of my first meeting with the all-women, all-star team at Crown Publishers, I got all misty and told them that I'd been *waiting for them my whole life*. They were worth the wait. **Tina Constable, Sarah Breivogel, Tammy Blake, Meredith McGinnis,** and **Jennifer Reyes** are simply the best. And I will be ever grateful to **Mary Choteborsky,** who was like a lantern for this flame, protecting and guiding it every step of the way. Her lucid and mindful editing not only made this more accessible, but will also influence everything I write from now on.

Lisa DiMona, my literary champion, is not only a savvy agent, but also a lovely human being. Proposal doctor **Linda Sivertsen** was the best cheerleader a weary author could hope for. Creative seer **Dyana Valentine** is the fiery voice of wisdom and "you can do it-ness" that I'd only faintly believed existed. **Rebecca Walker** was there when this was a seedling and helped me see how it could grow.

Alexandra Franzen, my wingwoman, made me aspire to her level of impeccability and soul shine. **Kris Carr** and **Marie Forleo** blew off the fog of doubt with their big visions and even bigger love. **Angie Wheeler** kept me wired and organized.

For contributing directly to this work, I am grateful to **Elizabeth Talerman** of Nucleus; **Michael Bungay Stanier,** author of *Do More Great Work;* and *The Art of Non-Conformity* author, **Chris Guillebeau,** for true friendship and sharing his playbook.

Dozens of well-prepared people wrote about or interviewed me and let me show up on their websites and shows talking about me, me, me. Thank you for the stage. My blog family at **LifeRemix.net** has been an incredible source of know-how and encouragement.

At one point or another, sometimes repetitively and very loudly, **Donna VanEvery, Navjit Kandola, Samantha Reynolds, Pete McCormack, Ishita Gupta, Jonathan Fields, Lee-Anne Ragan, Karis Hiebert, Dolly Hopkins, Michelle Pante, Tammy Mazak, Kelly Hoey, Joshua Pettinato, Adam Baker, Jonathan Mead, Chela Davison, Gabrielle Bernstein,** and **Kate Northrup** told me to *Rock the Fuck On!*

My **parents** brought to my attention that I always seem to pull it off and that this time would be no exception and that's all there is to it. **Dr. Diane Chung** made sure my chi went *cha-ching*. And **Michael Barden** made sure my soul went *cha cha cha*.

Stephanie Corker reminded me that it was a done deal. **Lianne Raymond** reminded me about the poetry of my calling. **Karen Lam** reminded me about High Magic. **Bindu Wiles** reminded me of the beauty of natural disasters. **Hiro Boga** reminded me of my future.

Candis Hoey reminds me almost daily that it's all pretty simple when you get right down to it.

My true love, **Scott,** held me in every way that one can be held—and never let go. This offering is founded in his steadfast ways and could not have happened so surely without him. We have a magic son. He asked me, "Mama, why are you writing a book if I can't read yet?" *Because my heart* has *to write it. Feels good. I know you'll have that feeling someday.*

And **You**! Holy smokes . . . **You.** Thank you so very, very much for being here. Namasté.

THE
SONIC FIRE
PLAYLIST

The following music was listened to obsessively while creating this book:

Imogen Heap, *Ellipse*

Hildegard von Bingen, *The Origin of Fire*

Glenn Gould, *Bach: The Two and Three Part Inventions*

Sade, *Soldier of Love*

Matisyahu, *Light*

Ben Harper, *Lifeline*

Jann Arden, *Free*

Erykah Badu, *New Amerykah, Part 2*

Metric, *Fantasies*

Alicia Keys, *The Element of Freedom*

Michael Franti and Spearhead, *The Sound of Sunshine*

k.d. lang, *Recollection*

Ray LaMontagne, *Gossip in the Grain*

Melody Gardot, *My One and Only Thrill*

Adele, *21*

Antony and the Johnsons, *I Am a Bird Now*

Florence + The Machine, *Lungs*

Balanescu Quartet, *Maria T*

CocoRosie, *Rainbowarriors*

Jason Mraz, *We Sing. We Dance. We Steal Things.*

Red Hot Chili Peppers, *I'm with You*

SPREAD THE FIRE

If you've been informed, inspired, or, like, rocked to the depths by *The Fire Starter Sessions,* here are some easy, good karma ways to help spread the fire, any of which I will be wildly grateful for:

1. **Send me an email or video testimonial.** Include a link to your site and your Twitter or Facebook name if you like—it just may get some airplay. **danielle@daniellelaporte.com**
2. **Tweet!** Tweet out your love or quotes from the book with **@daniellelaporte** in your message and/or the **#FireSS** hashtag.
3. **Post quotes or reviews on Facebook.** Rent billboards. Sky-writing is still very effective.
4. **Review the book** on any online bookseller's site.
5. Do a book review on **your site.**
6. **Every article on DanielleLaPorte.com is up for grabs.** Feel free to republish or distribute (with credit, of course). If you add linkbacks, all the better.
7. **Start a Camp Fire, a Fire Starter Sessions group.** Don't be shy. Go to **TheFireStarterSessions.com.**
8. **Remind your soul sisters, brothers, and lovers that enlightenment is sexy.** And then hold up this book and wink wink. They'll get it.

now works

You're here for a reason.

And that reason is yours to define.

Make it something amazing and really full of love and things that feel hot.

Be unreasonable.

Be scared if you need to be.

Just keep moving.

Feeling.

Asking.

Don't take any shit, and for the love of God, please don't settle.

Just keep choosing.

Make lots and lots and lots of choices.

You are writing the movie script of your life.

Desire. Lights. Action! (Some tears.)

You're a hero on an adventure.

This is it. This is the adventure.

Creativity. Change. Livelihood. Art. People. Leadership. Legacy.

Score. Money. Gain. Failure. Pride. Industry. Simple. Love.

LOVE.

Oh, love.

It's all about love in the end.

And in the beginning.

So start now, today, here.

Let it be simple, easy, electric.

Be surprised, be new, be true, be you.

Now.